Commercial Real Estate: Demystified

How to PROFIT From Cash-Flowing Commercial Real Estate

Howard "Doc" Haller

Published by Silver Eagle Press, Coeur d'Alene, Idaho

ISBN: 1-60655-036-5
ISBN-13: 978-1-60655-36-6

CONTENTS

Chapter 1

It Is Easier to Purchase Commercial Real Estate Than It Is to Purchase a Home

Cash flowing commercial property can produce a significant passive income and increase your net worth, thereby, allowing you to be able to do the things you want, when you want, whether that's to become your own boss, pay off debt, put your kid (or yourself) through college, retire comfortably, go on luxury vacations, or buy that brand-new pacific blue Lexus you've been looking at.

There's a myth out there, that to invest in commercial real estate, you need tons of your own money, and perfect credit. But whether or not you have those things is not the real problem. . . . The real problem is you don't know the steps to take. You don't have the information you need, and you don't have anyone to answer your questions. That's what stops you from investing. You're scared. You are afraid. You're worried you're going to make a mistake. I understand; I used to feel that way too.

But I discovered the Truth, and there are simple, learnable steps that can help you become successful investing in commercial real estate.

So, allow me to debunk that myth that you need lots of your own money and perfect credit. No, you don't. When you know how to find the right cash flowing property, it becomes easier to buy commercial real estate than it is to buy a house. And the reason is, the property's NOI. NOI is Net Operating Income.

It's how much money a property makes, after all expenses. It's the money from all the rents from the tenants, whether it's an apartment building, an office building, or self-storage building. . . minus all the expenses, such as property tax, utilities, repairs and maintenance, and insurance. And it will cover the property manager, so you don't have to do the work. We'll also subtract the money needed to make the loan payments. Then, and this is the best part, all the money left over goes right into your bank account each and every month.

The lender looks at the NOI. If they know the property is making enough to pay their loan payment, along with the other expenses, then the lender is going to give you the loan you want. You see? The lender is looking primarily at the property's Net Operating Income. Not you. With commercial loans, you are not the primary source of repayment. This is why it is easier to buy commercial real estate than it is to buy a home.

Because we all know with a home loan, it's your money, your credit, and your debt ratios, and your take-home pay from your JOB. But with commercial, it's the property's NOI.

Learning the steps to invest in commercial real estate is the great equalizer. It does not matter who you are: your age, gender, race, religion, citizenship, employment status, if you're married, single, starting with lots of money, or just a little.

When you know how to find a great NOI deal, you are on your way to becoming financially free as a commercial real estate investor!

With my help, one of my mentee's, JD, who was only twenty-four years old (hadn't ever bought a home and was out of work), could buy a nine-unit apartment building that put over $1,773 into his bank account every month. He did not have a current paycheck. If he wanted to buy a house, he wouldn't have been able to because he had no take-home pay, but he could use this property's NOI as leverage to buy one.

When you get a loan for a house, the lender determines the ratio of the principal, interest, taxes, and insurance divided by your take-home pay. Guess what? He didn't have any take-home pay; therefore, he could not have bought a house. True? Absolutely! But he could buy the apartment because of the NOI. There's your answer of how this all works. I hope that this short illustration of a real case study helps you. We'll get deeper into NOI and other financial numbers in Chapter 16: Key Financial Ratios for Evaluating Income Properties.

This book is written for people like you—people who are curious about commercial real estate and how commercial real estate owners make money. It's for those who are intrigued about commercial real estate, but who are a bit apprehensive because of their lack of knowledge about what commercial real estate is, how it works, and what's involved.

Let's get started.

Chapter 2

What Is Commercial Real Estate?

Per the National Association of Realtors, commercial real estate is defined as "any multifamily residential, office, industrial, or retail property that can be bought or sold in a real estate market." This might seem straightforward, but there are a few additional intricacies to the commercial real estate market that differentiate it from the homeowner's market.

While it's easy to identify a commercial real estate property that's used as an office building, by definition, commercial real estate is any building or property that houses one or more retail businesses where the general public can go to purchase goods or services. There are also industrial commercial real estate properties that usually fall into the categories of distribution center, manufacturing facilities, or warehouses. And it includes specialty commercial real estate properties that may function as medical, office building, self-storage, five-plus unit apartments, hotels, motels, senior centers, golf courses, resorts, and more.

Commercial real estate can also be broken down into one of two categories: Owner occupied commercial properties and commercial investment properties. Owner occupied commercial real estate is just what you would probably assume it to be. It is a building that may house offices or some other type of business, such as manufacturing, and the building is owned by the main or primary tenant in the building. The reason we use the term "primary tenant" is that sometimes a company or business may buy a property, such as a large office building, and utilize most of the space in the building for their own purposes while renting out small sections of the building to other companies. In this case, the owner owns the entire building and is considered the primary tenant as well. The second category is non-owner occupied, which is any commercial building not occupied by the owner. Offices, apartments, industrial, retail, and other commercial properties fall into this category.

Aren't Residential and Commercial Real Estate the Same Thing?

The short answer to that question is "no." Residential real estate can be considered as real estate that provides domiciles or places for people to live. Commercial real estate involves any property that is purchased with the intent of making money through leasing the property to someone else or occupied by the owner. And, to clear up one point that confuses some people, there can be properties that people live in and are considered commercial real estate. An example of this would be a large apartment complex. But, by definition, a property such as a duplex, triplex, or a fourplex is not commercial real estate, even though the owner would be making money from leasing or renting the duplex, triplex, or fourplex units. The reason is that single family homes and small residential spaces up to four units have the same type of noncommercial real estate loans, called conforming loans. Residential with units of five or more, such as apartments, require a commercial loan, and as such are deemed commercial real estate.

Commercial real estate covers a lot of territory because it is ultimately the driving force behind a vibrant economy in many nations throughout the world.

Some Major Categories of Commercial Real Estate

Office Buildings

This category includes small and large office buildings, as well as single-tenant and multi-tenant properties and skyscrapers. This type of commercial property is specifically used for housing a business. There might be employees, staff, management, or basic office equipment contained within the piece of real estate, and this designation can apply to an entire building or just the floor of a building. Within office real estate, there are three classes: A, B, and C. Real estate classified as A is modern and up to date, while classes B and C may be older and not up to modern building standards. Usually, offices in class A have a higher rental value and have more amenities.

Industrial Properties

This category includes very large offices with warehouses and distribution/warehouse/distribution center properties. One of the most defining characteristics of industrial properties is the Clear Height. This refers to the height of the steel girders inside the interior. Smaller properties may have a Clear Height of fifteen feet while larger properties have a Clear Height above forty feet. Another characteristic of industrial properties is the number of docks it has and the type of docks. Grade Level Docks are when the warehouse floor and parking lot are located on the same level. Semi-Dock height is that of a delivery truck while Full-Dock height is the height of a semitruck.

While industrial real estate will also house employees and staff, the primary purpose of this type of commercial real estate is to provide a location for equipment and merchandise. The main purpose of industrial property will be for manufacturing, production, or distribution. Warehouses and distribution facilities are good examples of industrial real estate.

Multifamily/Apartments

Multifamily apartment buildings with five or more units are classified as "commercial real estate" for both financing and local tax purposes. Duplexes (two residential units), triplexes (three units), and fourplexes (four units), are classified as "non-commercial" by lenders rules and regulations. The reason duplexes, triplexes, and fourplexes are not viewed as commercial real estate is because they fall into the "conforming loan" category under FHA underwriting standards. Single family homes also fall in the same category of being a "conforming loan." However, for investment purposes, it is generally appropriate to refer to all apartments (five units and over) as commercial property.

Anything that is more than a fourplex is considered commercial multifamily real estate. The category also covers apartment complexes and any high-rise apartments.

Strip Shopping Centers and Retail Malls

As indicated by the name, retail property is that which is used to sell goods or services. This might be a boutique, a grocery store, an apparel business, or a travel agency. When considering this type of real estate, it's important to take into consideration the retail trade area, which refers to the area from which the business hopes to draw customers. Without a dependable retail trade area, the property is unlikely to profit.

These two categories cover the buildings themselves and the pad sites which are located on the front of a highway, strip shopping centers, large shopping centers, single-tenant retail buildings, anchor tenants, power centers, outlets, malls, etc.

Medical Office Buildings

This includes doctor's offices, surgical centers, medical office buildings, dental buildings, etc. Ownership is a good option for medical professionals and medical partnerships who can gain the major tax and financial benefits of owning their own building(s).

Self-Storage

The need continues for self-storage facilities to serve people's ongoing need to store property, park RVs, and much more.

Mobile Home Parks

Nearly 10 percent of the population of the U.S. lives in mobile home parks. Warren Buffett and his company, Berkshire Hathaway, have invested tens of billions of dollars into the industry.

Land

This category includes all rural and otherwise undeveloped land that will be used in the future for commercial or apartment development. It can also include a pad site or infill land.

For individuals and companies that own a business, it is common to buy the necessary commercial property when appropriate commercial real estate financing is available. The decision to do this is similar in some ways to a homeowner deciding to buy their house rather than rent it.

Differences Between Commercial and Residential Real Estate

Loans for commercial real estate properties are structured differently than residential home loans. Residential home loans are often for terms of thirty years (or sometimes fifteen years); commercial real estate loans are typically for much shorter periods (usually five to ten years, or fewer), with a twenty-year amortization. This way the lender can provide the financing for the commercial property, and, by requiring the buyer to refinance every five or ten years, the lender is not taking such a long-term large risk on a property that can be valued at a million dollars or much more.

Finally, in terms of term, rate, and underwriting, the mortgage for a commercial property is unlike that for a residential property. Apartment owners; homeowners; and duplex, triplex, and fourplex buyers can get a mortgage that's backed by a government organization, whereas the interest rate for a commercial property mortgage can be slightly higher.

To ensure the venture is successful, a buyer needs to have due diligence, financial analysis, and deal structure. Someone who is buying commercial real estate, has done his homework, and has the proper due diligence and research will be able to present to a lender that a prospective property will be a profitable deal and that the property will be able to amply pay the loan payment and more.

Chapter 3

What Are the Advantages of Owning Commercial Real Estate?

There are five basic reasons to own commercial real estate as an investment:

1. Incoming cash flow from tenant leases and NNN (triple net lease)
2. Tenant reimbursement for property taxes, insurance, repairs/maintenance
3. Pride of ownership: "I own a cash flowing nine-unit apartment building"
4. Equity built up through the property's appreciation in value
5. Principal reduction

If you have an investment portfolio and are looking for ways to diversify, are trying to add tax benefits on your personal or corporate taxes, or just want to build wealth for yourself and your personal estate, owning commercial real estate is a great option. However, experts in the field of commercial real estate will remind you that it is a business with some risks. There are protections for investors who do complete their due diligence properly. Commercial real estate investors need to make informed and intelligent business decisions. Many active successful investors are doing quite well and enjoying all the benefits that can come with owning commercial real estate; they are the people who did do their entire due diligence up front.

A popular discussion topic among both professional investors and financial experts is what long-term investment choices are best.

- What are the most important attributes of a successful strategy for long-term investing?
- Which opportunities offer the most advantages?
- Why does commercial real estate have such a stellar reputation in the professional investment community?
- Are there specific advantages for owning commercial real estate?

For various reasons, not everyone chooses to own commercial real estate. Some folks will have apprehensions about larger investments or will lack knowledge about commercial real estate. Some people who own commercial real estate do so because they want to generate a new source of cash flow or add to the cash flow vehicles they already have.

Buying commercial real estate can be a profitable investment, regardless of whether you are buying a commercial property to house your own business or as an investment with the intention of leasing all or part of it for short- or long-term. As it is with any kind of investment, purchasing or investing in commercial real estate requires you to do a lot of research, get reliable advice from experts in the commercial real estate field, and make sure you do what you can to understand the onslaught of risks and benefits. Remember; fall in love with the numbers.

What Are the Advantages of Commercial Real Estate Investments?

We will start with a summary of eleven primary advantages and then discuss each point in more detail.

- Higher income potential
- Lower vacancy risk
- Less competition
- More flexible sellers
- Depreciation tax shelter
- Expenses paid by tenants (reimbursements, aka Triple Net Lease NNN)
- Equity build-up
- Solid economic value
- Financial leverage
- Long-term capital appreciation
- Credit tenant leases

Before proceeding, a note about the "due diligence" process is in order. Smart investors should include this critical step in everything they do. This process refers to a thorough review and analysis of both facts and assumptions. For example, instead of accepting at face value the financial data and other property information provided by the seller, a due diligence review would include a series of reviews of the seller's information, the data from the County Government (County Tax Assessor, Building and Safety) and a local title company, a detailed financial review of the last three year's income and expenses, and the examination of the current rent roll and all the leases.

This critical area will often represent the most important milestones in any prudent investment analysis. It is also typically where commercial real estate experts earn their reputations for excellence and success in investing.

Commercial Property Advantages Due to Lower Vacancies

With commercial real estate investments, stable predictable income is one of the driving forces behind long-term success. One of the advantages of commercial real estate is that the vacancy risk is minimal.

During the selection and acquisition phase, professional property managers, in combination with the initial due diligence, will help reduce any potential vacancies. Commercial office buildings offer a combination of solid tenant leases, preferable with credit tenants (such as major companies with stable and strong financials)

Less Competition from Buyers and More Flexibility by Sellers

Commercial real estate has less competition because it's bigger, more complex, and out of many potential buyer's comfort zones. These potential buyers don't have the kind of knowledge that you are going to obtain by reading this book.

Each property has a specific location and identity. For those interested in purchasing business properties, it is possible to devote appropriate time and effort to a prudent level of due diligence before negotiating with sellers. When investors are ready to negotiate, they will typically find professional owners who understand the practical need to be flexible when discussing acceptable financial terms for selling, especially if the buyer's proposal about the advantages to the seller are clearly presented. Also, commercial real estate is not someone's home. There is less emotional attachment and sellers are in a business state of mind. Tax Depreciation and Expense Advantages with Commercial Real Estate

One of the best advantages involving commercial real estate is that increases in net income can come from many different directions. Two of these important income sources are tax deductions (especially depreciation) and several expenses that are paid by tenants rather than the property owner. For example, it is normal with a triple net lease for the tenant to assume total financial responsibility for real estate property taxes, building insurance, maintenance/repair expenses, and utilities.

Capital Appreciation and Equity Build-Up Advantages of Commercial Property

While commercial real estate values will fluctuate, inflation and supply/demand factors provide a strong source of positive momentum for increasing property values over the long term. By itself, this will produce an increasing equity ownership position (the difference between value and debt). But, to provide a further boost to equity, as mortgage payments are made by investors over a period of years, the debt position will decrease, and the equity will increase. Equity build-up and property value appreciation can be thought of as a two-pronged source of powerful financial factors working behind the scenes to steadily increase an investor's equity position. They are two of the best "silent partners" that any investor is likely to find, and both are common advantages and attributes associated with commercial real estate.

Credit Tenant Leases

Commercial real estate, such as offices, retail mall, and industrial properties, lend themselves to large major corporations including highly desirable "credit tenant" leases, such as publicly traded firms.

Commercial Real Estate Advantages Accruing from Leverage and Solid Economic Value

In commercial property, when the term "leverage" is used, it means the property is purchased with a 20 to 40 percent down payment, equaling a 60 to 80 percent leverage. This is just one reason why financial experts refer to the "massive leverage" that is possible with contemporary commercial property investments. Such financial leverage means that investors get 100 percent of the income from the property with low money down. While it is still possible to finance commercial real estate with a traditional institutional lender, it is also possible to get secondary seller financing. And, it is possible to get 100 percent of seller financing to bypass all institutional financing. It also means that 100 percent of the property value increases belong to the buyer regardless of how small the down payment was at the time of initial purchase.

Commercial real estate is a classic example of solid economic value. Commercial real estate in such forms as industrial property, office buildings, retail stores, self-storage, and apartment buildings is a vital part of a vibrant economy. Even with minimal inflation, the solid economic value only gets better.

Don't Go It Alone—Utilize Expert Advice to Guide You

Regardless of whether you're new to commercial real estate ownership, or you're experienced and already own one or more commercial real estate property, any time you choose to purchase commercial real estate you should always seek out advice and counsel from experts in the industry—whether it's in your own area or across the country. Find top notch commercial real estate agents or brokers, property managers, mortgage brokers, commercial real estate attorneys, and other key team members.

A commercial real estate mentor can teach you, guide you, and show you the "real world" of commercial real estate. Commercial real estate mentors can teach and show you:

- How to select a commercial property
- How to find commercial real estate properties
- How to get all the financial information
- How to analyze the numbers to ensure the deal makes sense
- How to negotiate with property owners (or their brokers)
- How to structure and finance a commercial real estate purchase
- How to complete the due diligence
- How to close the commercial real estate purchase

Sometimes people think they can do all the homework on their own without the help of a broker or a commercial real estate management company; however, it is wise to engage a knowledgeable "street smart" commercial real estate broker, agent, or mentor to assist you in finding properties, analyzing the data provided, structuring the purchase offer, conducting the due diligence, arranging financing, and closing the deal.

As a prospective commercial real estate owner, doing all the due diligence means you can rest easy at night, knowing your investment and ownership in a property is stable.

Chapter 4

Advantages and Disadvantages of Investing in Apartments

Apartments are one of the most popular forms of housing in the United States. In many large cities, apartments represent 40 percent of all housing. Of all commercial real estate, 25 percent or more are apartments. With apartments being this prominent, commercial real estate investors are likely to consider purchasing apartment properties. Are they a good investment? What are the advantages and disadvantages?

Apartment investments have enjoyed a special place in the hearts and wallets of many long-term investors. For anyone who has selected commercial real estate as a smart investment path to follow, what are the key advantages of investing in multi-unit real estate properties?

Advantages of Investing in Apartments

Apartments have provided one of the best overall returns among all types of commercial property during the past thirty years on a nationwide basis. There will, of course, be regional differences that show both better and worse results. Annualized returns for apartments range from 7.5 to 9 percent depending on which period is included. It is important to review and analyze the specific potential advantages for apartment investments.

Lower Costs

If you're thinking of buying a single-family rental or a ten-unit apartment building and have an unplanned vacancy, you should look at the cost per month. Let's look closer at what happens in the following scenarios:

Scenario 1: You own a single-family home as a rental. You have a one-month vacancy. The rent per month is $2,500 with a mortgage of $1,500. Because of the vacancy, the investor is going to pay $1,500 mortgage to the bank for the one-month vacancy while there is no money coming in.

Scenario 2: You own a ten-unit apartment building. You have a one-month vacancy.

In the first scenario, you can see that you lose 100 percent of your cash flow on your single-family home if your one renter moves out (especially damaging if the vacancy extends for a longer time), until you can find a new tenant.

In contrast, in the second scenario, when a ten-unit apartment has a single vacancy, it is still 90 percent occupied, thus you still acquire 90 percent of your cash flow from your rental. When it comes to vacancies, apartments have a much smaller risk than single-family homes.

Tax Benefits and Lower Down Payments for Apartments

When considering apartments, the solid stability of housing economics has resulted in the willingness of lenders to accept lower down payments as well as to provide longer loans for investors who are buying apartments—as opposed to those who are buying office buildings and specialized commercial real estate. Mortgage lending institutions know that individuals will always need to make living arrangements.

The availability of tax deductions for operating expenses, depreciation, and cost segregation are positive financial advantages that will enhance the economics for owning apartments.

Flexible Sellers and Less Competition for Apartments

Smart investors should always hope for less competition rather than more competition from other buyers. With apartments, reduced buyer competition is common and is a major advantage when viewed in combination with the typical flexibility of current owners who are selling.

Lower Vacancy Risk and Higher Income Potential for Apartments

Income projections for apartments are consistently stable as are many other categories of commercial real estate. Stability is highly desirable in any investment. Positive cash flow can contribute to equity build-up by enabling debt levels to be paid off more quickly. While apartment vacancies can and will occur, they represent a lower and more manageable financial risk relative to other commercial properties.

Other Advantages:

- Partial and up to 100 percent seller financing is common
- Demographic trends are favorable for growth and demand
- More stable income compared to single-family homes
- Regardless of the economy, everyone needs to live

somewhere

- Much easier to manage than multiple single-family houses
- Shorter leases than other forms of commercial real estate
- Rent adjustments are easier to make
- With effective property managers in place, apartments provide passive investor income
- Vacancy risks are lower and easier to control than single family houses
- Landlord-tenant rights are protected and defined by both State and Federal laws
- Financing for apartments is easier to obtain (with lower interest rates and longer terms) than mortgage loans for other types of commercial real estate
- Financial leverage is possible with lower down payments
- FHA (Federal Housing Administration) financing is often available for maximum leverage (20–25 percent down payments)
- Refinancing apartments with an FHA non-recourse, assumable loan (up to a thirty-five-year fixed rate loan) is an amazing advantage
- Federal and State housing programs provide financial support and stability
- Job insecurity, rising student debt levels, and the foreclosure crisis have each separately increased demand for apartments (this is expected to continue)
- Shorter construction and development cycle
- Long-term capital appreciation

- Equity build-up
- Economic value
- Tax benefits such as depreciation and cost segregation accounting
- Reduced competition from other investors, as compared to single family homes
- Increased potential for positive cash flow
- Residential tenants instead of business tenants (both good and bad at the same time)
- More apartment renters are now longer-term residents and less transient
- FHA does offer apartment construction loans (from the start of construction) that are fixed rate for thirty-plus years

Capital Appreciation and Leverage for Apartments

These first two advantages of investing in apartments real estate properties can be looked at separately, but they happen to complement each other very well. Long-term capital appreciation is depicted by the increasing value of the investment over a period of several years.

Property valuations can increase for many reasons such as inflation, increased demand, and shrinking supply. Leverage refers to borrowing a significant part of the purchase price. No money down and minimal down payments are examples of "massive leverage."

Apartments Economic Value and Equity Build-Up

Apartments represent solid economic value because they are tangible property that an owner can look at and touch. In comparison, common stock is a theoretical ownership interest that can change artificially without the possibility of touching what it represents at all. Will Rogers once famously said investors should do the following: "Buy land. They aren't making any more of it." While there are several variations of this timeless wisdom, the point not to be missed is that apartment ownership includes the purchase of a scarce commodity known as land.

Equity is the ownership position reflected by deducting mortgage debt from total value of the property. Equity can grow by either increases in value or reduction of the mortgage balance. When both happen at the same time, investors will experience the best example of equity build-up. This does not have to happen quickly to produce impressive financial results.

The importance of apartments exhibiting less sensitivity to the economy is especially relevant in comparison to other types of commercial real estate. As supply and demand changes, the ease of adjusting apartment rental prices provides an exceptional degree of flexibility that is unusual for other commercial property investment categories. Apartment rent rates are currently at a lifetime-high rate.

The final advantage noted above has particularly positive implications for apartment investing. The foreclosure crisis dislocated many individuals and families. Even if they want to buy a single-family home again, these former homeowners will not be eligible for traditional real estate financing for several years, in most cases. In the meantime, they need somewhere to live and apartments provide a solution. Residential rents have continued to increase in recent years.

By most estimates, each 1 percent reduction in homeownership represents another one million renters. A sluggish economy causes many individuals to relocate in search of employment opportunities.

Possible Disadvantages of Apartments

Apartment investments can involve a choice between new construction or buying existing apartments. Building new apartment properties involves additional risks and disadvantages not outlined below. For example, extensive marketing becomes an expense as well as a requirement with new properties. It is also difficult to forecast if there will be sufficient demand for a new construction apartment project.

Commercial development and apartment development is a time-consuming and complicated process. Such construction risks and uncertainties can be avoided when investors focus on the inventory of existing apartments.

Maintenance and Management Are Critical

Owning any rental property will involve work. But, if you hire an effective property manager, your personal involvement is reduced. With a single-family home, you usually deal with one tenant. With apartments, this is not the case. Even with the best tenants, some problems may arise. You must keep up with maintenance needs or your tenants will move out.

You may consider employing the services of a property management firm to help with the common rental issues (collecting rents, accounting, repair requests, etc.). Property management will impact your cash flow. Different property management firms charge a percentage of the actual rent collected, plus a commission on new rentals.

If you hire an effective property manager, he or she will save you a lot of time and headaches, will professionally manage your apartment, will ensure rents are collected, and will manage tenant issues.

Property managers will assist and help an apartment owner with:

- Eviction laws (which vary from state to state)
- Collecting rents (not always easy)
- Tenant turnover (which can quickly impact cash flow)
- Increasing rental competition (marketing strategies)
- Security deposits (rules vary by state)
- Leasing new rentals

With effective property management in place, many of the potential disadvantages can be reduced or eliminated. Finding and selecting a property manager is one of the most important goals for commercial real estate investors to achieve in their efforts to produce a successful apartment investment.

Location

Location is key when it comes to purchasing apartment units. Look for areas where rents are increasing, which is a good indication of potential increased value of the building as well. Make it a priority to know the market value; get the historical and current numbers and get the actual Net Operating Income information!

Chapter 5

How Are Apartments Different from Other Commercial Real Estate Investments?

There are major differences between apartments and other kinds of commercial real estate.

- Residential tenants
- Shorter tenant leases
- Federal, State, and local laws for landlords and tenants
- Federal and State housing agencies
- No triple net leases
- Better availability of construction financing rates and terms
- More attractive financing terms for permanent financing
- Easier to manage and understand
- Lower down payment requirements and, therefore, more leverage

With each individual apartment investment opportunity, there is likely to be a unique set of circumstances. Commercial real estate investors should always exercise an appropriate level of due diligence regardless of what type of property is being evaluated. As shown above, a prudent financial planning process should anticipate both the similarities and the differences that will be encountered in any comparison of apartments with other commercial properties.

Despite the many advantages of commercial real estate in comparison with other investment alternatives, all commercial properties are not created equal. There are distinct differences among the most popular categories of multifamily apartments, industrial properties, retail buildings, and office complexes. Apartments might represent the most unique variation of commercial real estate. The differences between apartments with five or more units and other types of commercial real estate (warehouses and offices, for example) are even more striking when specialized businesses (such as golf courses and restaurants) are included in the analysis.

Residential Tenants Instead of Business Tenants

One of the most striking differences is that apartments represent a place to live rather than a place to work or conduct business activities. The absence of business tenants makes apartments especially unique when compared to other types of commercial real estate.

Shorter Leases More Common

Apartment leases are frequently month-to-month or are for fixed periods of one to two years. Business leases for other commercial properties are typically for longer terms (although month-to-month agreements still exist) such as five to ten years or more. This key difference allows apartment investors to generally avoid being locked in to previous market leases during periods when apartment rents are rising.

Specific, Helpful Local, State, and Federal Laws

The legal guidelines for multifamily housing facilitate a smooth relationship between residents and property managers. Some of the most influential legislation (such as Section 8) enables low-income tenants to receive federal government subsidies for their monthly housing expenses. These programs are federally funded, but locally administered by the Local Housing Authority.

Federal Agencies Dedicated to Management of Housing Programs

The U.S. Department of Housing and Urban Development (HUD) is a major federal agency dedicated to helping both tenants and property owners in a variety of ways. Many special housing programs are coordinated by the Federal Housing Administration (FHA). The Federal (and state) housing agencies help to create and sustain a positive and growing demand for housing services. HUD funds and oversees the local Housing Authority programs including the Section 8 program.

Absence of Triple Net Leases

In many commercial real estate investments, it is often common for business tenants to sign a triple net lease (NNN) in which they assume their prorated portion of the total financial responsibility for building repair and maintenance, insurance, and property taxes. With apartments, it is common for residential tenants to assume responsibility for paying for some or all of their individual utility expenses, but apartment investors will routinely be responsible for ***all*** property tax payments, insurance, and maintenance expenses.

Construction Financing Is More Accessible

In recent years, the real estate and construction industry has been experiencing some minor irregularities and lack of normal financing availability for many commercial properties. However, apartments have enjoyed a steady funding pipeline due in part to the unique aspects of housing economics and specialized construction financing from the Federal Housing Administration (FHA).

Better Financing Terms

Financing for most commercial real estate is more difficult to obtain and more expensive than loan terms for apartments. It is not unusual for many traditional commercial loans to be limited to periods of ten to twenty years for business properties other than multifamily housing. With apartments, it is not unusual to find thirty-year-loan terms readily available. Lower interest rates and fixed rate loans are also commonly offered to apartment investors.

Traditional business loans for many commercial properties also often have restrictive loan covenants such as prohibiting the assumption of an existing loan by a new buyer. In direct contrast, FHA financing terms may permit Assumable Loans and Non-Recourse refinancing. This allows much more flexibility when apartment owners are negotiating with prospective sellers.

Easier to Understand and Manage

Many individuals (including investors) have more first-hand knowledge of apartments than they do about other types of commercial property. This is due to either having lived in apartment complexes or visiting friends who live in multi-unit properties or apartments.

Managing apartments is also usually less complicated than managing specialized commercial properties. The skills to manage one apartment property are easily transferable to other multifamily units. This is not always the case with other types of commercial real estate.

Smaller Down Payments and Higher Leverage

Due to the ability to make a smaller down payment, apartment investors will find that more leverage is possible with multifamily housing investments. For example, with many FHA loan programs, it is possible to acquire financing for up to 92.5 percent of the purchase price if a secondary loan (such as seller financing) is used in the purchase.

Shorter Depreciation Schedule

Residential income property, which includes single-family homes, two- to four-unit complexes and apartments, has a 27.5-year straight line deprecation length. Other commercial real estate has a 39-year deprecation term. Residential income properties are also an excellent candidate for cost segregation options under the U.S. IRS Code. Cost segregation allows an investor to break down the components of the apartment building such as furniture, appliances, fixtures, and other components that have a shorter deprecation schedule in order to maximize the tax benefit of quicker tax write-off.

One of the advantages to owning apartment real estate is the higher likelihood of always having potential tenants. In other words, apartments are potentially always profitable if managed correctly. Also, apartment real estate is always easier to sell than commercial real estate property. Apartment real estate is valuated per the prices of similar buildings, in the same area, with similar characteristics.

Banks usually offer mortgages of 70 percent to 80 percent for apartments, so a buyer is only required to invest a smaller amount up front. However, a commercial appraisal, usually done by a Member of the Appraisal Institute (MAI) uses a three-approach system to value the property: 1) Net Operating Income (NOI of the subject property), 2) recent relative sales of similar properties, and 3) cost (replacement cost minus depreciation). As is true in other commercial real estate, the focus is on the NOI.

Commercial real estate property prices are higher, and the banks are willing to give smaller Loan-to-Value (LTV) loans than they are to apartment real estate. Commercial loans are mostly 60 percent of the property's value, since there is a larger financial risk for commercial real estate other than apartments.

While a financial institution may offer 60 to 82 percent LTV for commercial real estate and apartments respectively, the actual loan amount may be reduced to make sure the property can easily service the proposed debt. Lenders need to have an apartment's net operating income (NOI) to be able to generate 120 to 130 percent or more NOI to cover the loan payment. The 120 to 130 percent ratio is called the Debt Service Coverage Ratio (DSCR). For example, if the proposed monthly loan payment is $10,000, then the lender will require $12,000 or more NOI to provide the financial institution with adequate and excess DSCR. Commercial real estate, other than apartments, has a higher DSCR of 140 percent or more and a traditional LTV of around 60 percent.

Investors who are just starting out will often put their money into an apartment complex first and then turn to commercial properties once they have gained experience in different markets and will then acquire more knowledge pertaining to the different forms of investment properties.

Chapter 6

Why Should Investors Consider Apartments?

Commercial real estate, especially apartment properties, offers a wide assortment of sound choices for prudent investments. Over a period of several decades, investing in commercial property has proven to be a winning financial strategy. While historical returns are informative, most practical investors are more interested in the future.

Summary: Advantages of Apartments

- Long-term capital appreciation
- Financial debt leverage
- Equity build-up
- Economic value
- Lower down payments
- Long-term fixed rate financing
- Possible non-recourse and assumable loan
- Tax benefits such as depreciation (including cost segregation)
- Reduced competition from other investors
- Seller flexibility (better financial terms)
- Reduced vacancy risks
- Increased potential for positive cash flow

If an investor decides to focus on apartment real estate, an additional major benefit is that the above list of advantages for buying multifamily housing properties is equally applicable to all the apartment choices available to investors.

Please keep in mind that any investment should be analyzed from the perspective of intermediate to long-term, rather than from performance rate over the next few months or years. The future for commercial real estate looks promising in all the primary directions: multifamily housing (apartments), retail and restaurants, industrial properties, self-storage, mobile home parks, and office buildings. Some commercial real estate investors are more comfortable focusing on one or two of these areas. The analysis will provide a forward-looking view of what makes different types of apartments deserving of undivided attention from demanding investment professionals.

Apartment investments have enjoyed a special place in the hearts and wallets of long-term investors. For anyone who has selected commercial real estate as a smart investment path to follow, what are the key advantages of investing in multi-unit real estate properties?

Most institutional lenders will want to see a down payment, but a direct loan from commercial property owners may allow very low or no down payment financing (seller financing).

If an apartment property is purchased with all cash (no debt whatsoever), then there is no leverage (100 percent down payment). If the apartment value increases by 10 percent during any period, the rate of return on the investment is the same 10 percent. If an investor starts with a 10 percent down payment, the same 10 percent increase in value now produces a 100 percent rate of return (a little higher, but 100 percent reflects an adjustment for the cost of debt).

Tax Benefits and Lower Down Payments for Apartment Investments

When talking about apartment variations (five to hundreds of units), the solid stability of housing economics has resulted in the willingness of lenders to accept lower down payments. Loans for apartment are longer in comparison than those for office buildings and other commercial real estate.

The availability of tax deductions for net operating expenses and, especially, for depreciation is another positive financial advantage that will enhance the economics for owning apartments.

Flexible Sellers and Less Competition for Apartment Properties

Smart apartment investors should always hope for less competition from single-family residential buyers.

Chapter 7

The Advantages and Disadvantages of Investing in Office Buildings

When someone refers to commercial real estate, often the first image that pops into an investor's head is that of an office building. Office buildings are a popular type of commercial real estate and have some distinct advantages over apartment complexes and industrial real estate (like warehouses or self-storage).

Advantages of Office Buildings

One of the biggest advantages of investing in office buildings is that you're dealing with a professional business arrangement. If you aim to treat investing like a business, it's much easier to do so with office tenants than with residential tenants. You will be leasing to corporations, accountants, doctors, business owners, lawyers, and financial professionals. You also enjoy the benefit of a longer-term lease, usually around five to ten years, which means you can potentially worry less about constant turnover and vacancy.

Another advantage is the possibility of getting a triple net lease (NNN). An NNN is where you lease a property and get the tenant to pay not just the rent, but also 100 percent of their portion of the property taxes, insurance, utilities, and repairs and maintenance costs associated with your property. This isn't possible with residential properties, such as apartments.

One major irritation people have with residential property is the need to be on-call twenty-four hours a day, in the event of emergency. Office buildings are usually only occupied during work hours, meaning you can manage them during the day and have your nights to yourself.

Other Advantages:

- Investors can start small with small office buildings
- Institutional investors can participate with larger investment properties
- Seller financing (up to 100 percent) is possible
- Demographic trends are favorable for growth and demand
- More stable income in comparison with most other commercial properties
- Much easier to manage than multiple single-family houses or apartments
- Longer leases than apartment real estate
- With property managers in place, commercial real estate provides passive investor income
- Vacancy risks are lower and easier to control
- The tenants pay 100 percent of their prorated portion of the building's operating expenses (triple net lease)
- Possible SBA 504 loan for owner-user (up to 90 percent LTV loans)
- Long-term capital appreciation
- Equity build-up
- Economic value
- Tax benefits such as depreciation

- Reduced competition from other investors
- Increased potential for positive cash flow
- Business tenants instead of residential tenants
- Typically, office tenants have longer-term leases and less turnover

Office Building Economic Value and Equity Build-Up

An office building's owner's equity can be affected by two main factors:

1. The principal balance of the mortgages being reduced by the periodic monthly loan payments
2. The value of the office building could increase by increasing the office building's rents, which increases the Net Operating Income (NOI)

Disadvantages of Office Buildings

As enticing as the benefits of office buildings are, they aren't without some drawbacks. First, you need to get financing, and the commercial loan process is more complicated than that of residential loans. It's all about the numbers on the proposed deal of the office building, so you need a solid NOI to get loans. You will rarely get into a commercial property without 20 to 40 percent cash or more for a down payment, unless you get seller financing, mezzanine debt, or bring in a partner.

Investing in office buildings can involve a choice between buying new construction or buying existing office building properties. Constructing new office buildings involves additional risks and disadvantages. For example, extensive marketing becomes an added expense and requirement with new properties. It is also difficult to forecast if there will be sufficient tenant demand for a new office building project.

Is It Worth It?

Commercial office space can be a highly lucrative business, it depends on factors like your chosen location, the kind of tenants you have, and the physical conditions of the property. With the proper due diligence and the solid advice of a team of professionals, you will likely make good money in office buildings, but expect this to be an intermediate if not long-term investment.

Chapter 8

Advantages and Disadvantages of Investing in Industrial Real Estate

Both new and seasoned investors have been using commercial real estate as a central piece of their investment portfolio for several decades. However, with so many kinds of commercial property, how should choices for investing be made? Is one type of commercial real estate better than another?

The short answer: Each category of commercial real estate has its own advantages and disadvantages. Individual investors should consider their investment preferences and compare these to the pros and cons of each property type. This overview will focus on industrial real estate.

What Does Industrial Real Estate Include?

There are several business activities that can take place in industrial buildings. Here are some common examples:

- Research
- Warehousing
- Assembly
- Manufacturing
- Storage
- Production
- Distribution

The ability to perform the above activities will often be subject to local restrictions such as zoning and environmental regulations. With these categories of industrial facilities, it's apparent that significant differences exist between each one. The activities that will take place in a storage facility are distinctly different from what takes place in a manufacturing plant.

Even when focusing on manufacturers, there are distinctions between "light" and "heavy" manufacturing. Examples of heavy manufacturing include chemicals, plastics, steel, mining, and ship-building. In comparison, light manufacturing is frequently associated with using less raw materials and producing smaller consumer items, such as shoes, clothes, and furniture.

Advantages of Investing in Industrial Properties

There are several significant advantages to be realized by a commercial real estate investor who chooses to include industrial real estate in his or her investment portfolio.

- Seller financing (all or partial) may be available
- Extensive capital investment barriers to competition entering the market quickly
- Portfolio diversification due to potential for participation in international commerce
- Specialized industrial property investments involve less buyer competition
- Possible triple net leases can reduce financial risks (most industrial properties are leased on a "modified gross lease" not an NNN) so the owner pays some or most of the expenses

- Possible high-profile investment in local communities due to job benefits
- Stable cash flow with long-term leases and long-term tenants
- Support for other investments, such as apartments, by creating jobs and potential renters
- Tenants who are (often) well-known industrial companies and other financially-strong businesses (maybe a "credit tenant")
- Extensive financial support provided by economic development programs

With entire proper due diligence, investing in industrial properties can be sufficiently profitable to offset potential disadvantages. Perhaps more importantly, some of the possible advantages noted above can be enhanced by active involvement on the part of each industrial property owner. As one key example, there is specialized economic development support in many states and local jurisdictions that can provide significant hidden financial support for some industrial real estate projects. The economic incentives can take various forms and often include special long-term property tax exemptions, infrastructure subsidies, industrial revenue bonds (for long-term financing), and job credits.

In other situations, economic development agencies can actively provide marketing and public relations support that enables outreach to foreign corporations as potential future tenants and clients. While many of these industrial development programs are readily available, they require substantial initiative by industrial property owners.

When and if available, triple net leases (NNN) or modified gross leases (where the tenant pays part of the expenses) for industrial property tenants can remove substantial financial risks from the investment by requiring the tenant to pay for one or more of the following: property taxes, building insurance, utilities, property upkeep, and/or property improvements. In combination with a long-term lease, such terms can remove several of the potential disadvantages previously noted.

Owners of industrial properties often enjoy a high-profile community position by the perceived economic benefits from industrial activities. In a political and economic environment in which creating jobs is a "priceless" commodity, buying and owning industrial real estate can also have some "priceless" advantages.

Disadvantages of Industrial Real Estate Investments

The types of buildings and activities associated with industrial properties lead to most of the potential investment disadvantages. As with many other business activities, problems and disadvantages can also produce opportunities for turning a loss into a gain when managed appropriately. Due diligence for commercial real estate is always important.

- Modified Gross Lease
- Environmental issues and legal liabilities
- More complex insurance (often due to environmental coverage)
- Limited industrial property inventory
- Sensitivity to economic factors beyond investor control (import/export, business inventories, and foreign

currency fluctuations)

- Availability of financing more limited for single-use buildings
- Limited resale options for customized industrial facilities

In comparison to other types of commercial real estate, environmental regulations and conditions are likely to play a much larger role during the due diligence process. While manufacturing plants will almost always have environmental issues to some degree, other types of industrial property can have their own unique environmental problems. For example, issues with a storage facility can be created by a prior history of what was stored there. Beyond the potential disadvantage involving environmental and legal liabilities, the other potential problems are relatively minor in comparison.

Chapter 9

Advantages and Disadvantages of Investing in Strip Shopping Centers

Strip shopping centers or strip malls are also known as neighborhood centers and community centers. Compared to large shopping malls, these types of properties are located almost everywhere. Per the New York Times, there are currently 685 super-regional malls while the total for strip shopping centers is about 66,000.

The traditional open-air (non-enclosed) arrangement for a strip mall includes a row of three to twelve retail establishments. These numbers can vary (especially in larger community centers) along with the shape (straight, L-shaped, and C-shaped are most prevalent), and all stores typically open into one shared parking lot. Larger versions may have one or two anchor tenants such as grocery stores or a big-box retailer.

Unlike regional shopping centers/malls that often serve customers coming from twenty to fifty miles away, strip shopping centers rely on business from those living or working within about five miles. Neighborhood centers usually range from 5,000 to 100,000 square feet and serve customers in a three-mile radius. Community centers are larger (100,000 to 350,000 square feet) and draw their business from three to five miles away.

What are the advantages and disadvantages for investors thinking about a commercial real estate investment in strip shopping centers?

Advantages of Investing in Strip Shopping Centers

The most profitable investments involving strip shopping centers will be those that take advantage of changes in retail shopping habits. As with other commercial real estate investments, specialized retail properties can avoid most common disadvantages. A focus on fast casual dining has proven to be one visible example of a retail strategy that is frequently less sensitive to both the economy and internet shopping trends. Some neighborhood centers have chosen to specialize in health-related areas (fitness centers, yoga studios, massage, and day spas), while others have adopted a strategy of assorted activities (daycare, karate, crafts, and ballet). In all cases, the key to investment success for a strip shopping center is having several businesses that keep customers coming back on a regular basis, which would include convenient stores, drycleaners, and liquor stores.

Some of the Advantages of a Strip Mall Investment Property:

- Lessees pay the owner a bonus percentage rent if sale volume is higher than the base or the percentage rent could begin from the first dollar of their sales
- Seller financing may be available (all or partial financing)
- Practical investment options for smaller investors
- Limited new construction, so inventory is limited to available retail space

- Retail "percent lease" kickers just as large shopping centers do
- Triple net leases (NNN)
- Reimbursements of Common Area Maintenance (CAM)
- Lease length that are usually shorter than those in larger malls, making it easier to changes tenants and lease terms and rates
- Less competition from larger investors
- Easier to manage than larger shopping centers
- Strip mall shopping activities often involve necessities and daily needs
- Retail stores in higher-income areas experience less fluctuation in business activity
- Economic development assistance available for improvements and infrastructure
- Less seasonal activity than larger shopping malls
- If specialized, less cash flow volatility
- Reduced property taxes due to sales taxes generated by retail businesses
- Troubled properties will usually be undervalued, even in desirable locations
- An effective property manager can overcome most disadvantages

Potential Disadvantages of a Strip Shopping Center

As with any investment, entire full due diligence is an important ingredient for long-term financial success. For investments involving strip malls, this should include an examination of how retail shopping trends are changing.

- Tenants tend to be smaller businesses with less financial strength
- Strip shopping centers have an average vacancy rate of 10 percent compared to 8 percent for the larger regional shopping malls
- An empty storefront is more obvious when there are only a few businesses
- Absence of anchor tenants makes a business mortgage more difficult
- Competition provided by internet shopping has impacted businesses that are often located in strip shopping centers
- Retail shopping can fluctuate based on local employment and the economy
- With fewer tenants, one or two vacancies can quickly impact cash flow

Property management, when done effectively, can reduce or eliminate many of these potential risks. Reviewing existing lease agreements for current tenants during the due diligence process can address many potential concerns.

Because strip shopping centers serve a focused operating radius of three to five miles, forward-thinking investors can effectively coordinate several commercial real estate investment properties in the same area. For example, improvements in a strip shopping center owned by an investor are also likely to be a positive factor in nearby residential homes and apartments.

Chapter 10

Advantages and Disadvantages of Retail Shopping Centers

Shopping at retail stores is a regular activity for many of us. However, how we do this has changed over the years. The "general store" was often the only practical shopping solution until Henry Ford demonstrated that choices were possible with both cars and shopping habits. Since then, retail shopping has changed and become more specialized.

Today's shopping centers are a unique combination of many commercial enterprises that are managed as one property.

Retail Shopping Centers Can Be Categorized in Several Ways, Such as the Following:

- Regional shopping centers (under one million square feet of rentable space)
- Super regional shopping malls (over one million square feet)
- "Power Centers" (consisting only of "big box stores")
- Mixed-use town centers (combination of retail and residential spaces)
- Outlet malls (comprise many national brands sold at cheaper prices)
- Strip shopping centers (row(s) of retail stores opening into a common parking lot)

The concept of shopping centers is an ancient one. The beginning can be traced back at least 1,000 years when the Grand Bazaar in Iraq included multiple vendors. In the United States, the first shopping center (The Arcade) was developed in Rhode Island eighty-five years ago.

For several decades, "going to the mall" (which usually refers to the first two categories above) for individuals of all ages has been a favorite for shopping and entertainment. Demographic and economic trends have changed, but retail shopping centers are still prominent elements on the commercial landscape. "Big box stores" have provided a new and popular retail experience for many shoppers, and the retail shopping experience is still changing.

How should a commercial real estate investor view shopping centers as a potential investment? What are the advantages and disadvantages?

Advantages of Retail Shopping Centers

Retail shopping centers represent unique properties that are an essential part of retail/commercial activity in any community. Because a shopping mall of any size is likely to be a prominent feature in a town, owners of these commercial properties will be highly visible in the public eye.

Primary Investment Advantages for a Shopping Center Investment:

- Less buyer competition
- Eligibility for economic development funds to improve infrastructure and buildings
- Possible availability of seller financing

- Intermediate to long-term leases (two, three, five, or more years)
- Rent kickers in addition to rent; tenants pay a percentage of their sales in the form of additional rent to the landlord
- Tenants pay their prorated portion of the shopping centers' Common Area Maintenance (CAM)
- Possible property tax abatements as a result of sales tax generated by shopping centers
- High-profile properties
- Potential to start with small strip shopping centers, then move up to larger centers
- Reduced risks and cash flow volatility as a result of mixed-use variations
- Positive influence on other investments (such as apartments) when in close proximity to shopping centers
- Potential for tenants to be well-known businesses (credit tenants)
- Undervalued and troubled retail properties can provide exceptional opportunities for investing (could include retail properties with high vacancy rates)

Retail shopping centers represent one of the best illustrations regarding the combined importance of a thorough due diligence process and ongoing property management expertise. Even when commercial real estate investors are successful in purchasing a retail shopping center property at a bargain price, the best long-term investment results will require vigilance in managing the property effectively. When done properly, "going to the mall" can be a winning financial strategy.

Potential Disadvantages of Retail Shopping Centers

Commercial real estate investors should never lose sight of the basic economic laws involving supply and demand. When considering new construction, determine if there will be enough demand to support the new shopping center.

Larger shopping centers can be very profitable when managed effectively, but in most areas, there is currently not enough growth potential to support a new (traditional) regional or super regional shopping mall. During the last five years, about thirty-five outlet malls have been built in the United States, while only a few large traditional shopping centers have been developed.

- Retail stores of all kinds are very sensitive to local and national economic and employment conditions
- Internet shopping provides a cheaper and more convenient shopping alternative for many retail products
- Strict rules by property managers can discourage some stores from signing or renewing leases
- The mix of stores must be carefully considered in terms of competition for existing stores
- Retail leases with rates based upon a percentage of sales can result in cash flow fluctuations
- Retail sales activity can be seasonal in some states
- Empty stores are easily visible to shoppers and can result in negative impressions
- Without a partner, larger shopping centers do not provide realistic investment opportunities for average investors because of their cost and scope

- Without an anchor tenant(s), traditional commercial financing is difficult to obtain

Some potential disadvantages can be converted into an investment opportunity with the proper due diligence and with the help of effective property managers. The key to potential income improvements will be discovered during the due diligence process, prior to finalizing a property purchase.

Chapter 11

Advantages and Disadvantages of Investing in Self-Storage Units

Self-storage can be an excellent opportunity that many new investors completely overlook. It's different than what you traditionally think of as commercial real estate, like apartments, retail, or office space, but it has its merits.

Self-storage units first appeared in the United States over fifty years ago, but most of the growth in this vital commercial real estate sector has occurred during the last two decades. Self-storage unites seem to be everywhere, but are they a good investment?

What are the advantages and disadvantages of this specialized form of commercial property?

A Few Facts about Self-Storage

By at least one measure (Bloomberg Riskless Return Rankings), self-storage units provided the best risk-adjusted return among all real estate investment trusts (REIT) during the ten-year period ending in 2012. Investing in an REIT is not the same as buying a self-storage unit facility, but the Bloomberg data does provide valuable insights about the economics and profits for this type of commercial real estate. As with any analysis based on prior results, past performance should never be used as the basis for forecasting future outcomes.

Per the U.S. based Self-Storage Association, here are some additional facts that are relevant for potential self-storage unit investors:

- Average revenue per square foot is $1.12 for facilities without climate control ($1.42 for those with climate control) and an average facility has 46,000 square feet.
- Approximately 9 percent of U.S. households rent at least one unit in a self-storage facility (up from 6 percent eighteen years ago).
- People living in condos or apartments make up 27 percent of self-storage renters.
- Most customers rent storage units despite having other storage options such as a garage (65 percent), basement (33 percent), or attic (47 percent).
- Recent nationwide occupancy rates stand at 85 percent.

The "traditional" storage business was created in 1889 by the Bekins family and later became the Bekins Moving and Storage Company. As Americans became more mobile, their needs changed. This eventually led to the creation of a new kind of commercial real estate known as self-storage units.

The description "self-storage" is based upon a shortened version of "self-service storage."

Advantages of Investing in Self-Storage Units

First, self-storage is a commercial investment that shares many of the advantages with other investments—advantages such as leverage, favorable tax treatment, passive income, and appreciation. However, demand for storage space is often high, which makes it easier to operate at high occupancy.

As for the occupancy itself, you are spreading the risk to have so many units available for rent, as opposed to those who rent out a commercial office with just a few tenants. You also can offer other products and services for additional profit, like truck rental, locks, boxes, supplies, and more.

Self-storage also benefits from cheaper development costs than comparable commercial real estate like apartments or offices, sometimes up to 50 percent cheaper. And it's cheaper to operate and maintain the self-storage facility. Another major benefit of self-storage investment is the fact that it's mostly on month-to-month rentals, which gives you the ability to adjust rents as needed. Unlike retail space, demand for self-storage doesn't change dramatically based on the economy, and could in fact benefit from a recession, as more people downsize and turn to storage to hold their possessions.

Potential Advantages to Invest in Self-Storage Units:

- Seller financing (all or partial) may be available (If you don't ask, you don't get)
- Serves a combination of business and individual customers. On average, 30 percent of self-storage renters are businesses
- Warehouses, supermarkets, and other older buildings can be converted into storage units
- Storage units can be part of a multi-use property including retail, office, or industrial space
- Individual Demand: Per U.S. Census Data, approximately 40 million people move each year
- Business Demand: more companies are downsizing their physical spaces and need storage space for inventory and archived records

- Delinquency process is faster in comparison to apartments and generally permits prompt evictions and auctioning of contents to cover indebtedness
- No current rent regulations covering rates charged by self-storage facilities
- Expenses for maintenance and repairs are minimal
- Limited need for capital improvements
- Relatively easy to manage
- Low liability insurance rates because of reduced on-site activity (and often restricted access)
- Most renters have month-to-month agreements and rents can be adjusted without restrictions that are caused by longer leases
- Expense ratio (40 to 45 percent of gross revenues is common) creates attractive profit potential
- Higher capitalization rate than most other commercial property (about 2 percent higher yield or "cap rate" than apartments, industrial, and retail properties)
- High number of renters reduces risk and cash flow volatility when vacancies do occur
- Works well in proximity to apartments (a good investment fit for apartment investors)

Potential Disadvantages of Self-Storage Units

Of course, there are still some disadvantages of self-storage to keep in mind. Because of the many advantages, it has become a competitive industry. Appropriate full and complete due diligence is essential. Location in terms of proximity to potential users and ease of access is of critical value for improving occupancy rates. For investors considering purchase of land and construction of a new facility, it is especially important to review vacancy rates at potential competitors' storage properties. Unless competing facilities have occupancy rates of at least 90–95 percent, there might not be sufficient demand to support more self-storage units in the immediate area.

You simply must do your full and complete due diligence and evaluate competition, local economic conditions, management costs, and more. As prices climb on the best facilities and as customers demand more security from their self-storage facility of choice, it gets harder to afford a competitive self-storage investment.

Other disadvantages include:

- Legal lien laws on stored property varies from one state to another
- On-site management is required in many cases unless it is an automated facility
- Success of new properties depends on marketing and competition
- Some areas have very little vacant land to build new facilities
- Obtaining zoning approval can be difficult in some areas

With proper (or automated) management, this can be an investment that makes money for you without too much time invested. You also must contend with the potential for liability, if someone's possessions are lost, stolen, or damaged. That means you'll need a liability insurance policy, which is a normal tax deduction expense.

Three of the potential disadvantages for self-storage units apply only to new construction situations (buying vacant land, obtaining zoning approval, and marketing of new properties). For investors contemplating acquisition of existing self-storage unit facilities, potential disadvantages are much more limited and manageable.

Is It Worth It?

The financials will tell you if a self-storage opportunity is worth it. Because of the low maintenance costs and high profit potential, self-storage can be a fantastic investment. That means there could be competition, and you'll need to do the proper entire due diligence process before you pull the trigger and buy a self-storage facility.

Chapter 12

Advantages and Disadvantages of Investing in Mobile Home Parks

Purchasing a mobile home park is one of several commercial real estate investment strategies that involve the housing market. Other primary alternatives include multi-unit housing properties such as apartments. Potential investors in mobile home parks should evaluate the unique advantages and disadvantages.

The terminology for mobile home parks has changed over the years and involves an evolution from "trailer parks" to "manufactured homes" and "mobile home communities." Building and manufacturing standards have also improved during the last twenty-five years, and lingering impressions of "trailer homes" are no longer accurate when evaluating modern mobile home parks. Some of the misunderstandings and mistaken assumptions have created what prudent investors consider to be undervalued commercial real estate investments in regards to the low costs and supply/demand factors.

For example, Warren Buffett has a well-deserved stellar reputation when it comes to choosing profitable long-term investments. Two of his recent comments about investing in housing properties are that they represent "a very attractive asset class" and a "leveraged way of owning a very cheap asset." Warren Buffet's company, Berkshire Hathaway, owns the largest mobile home manufacturing company, as well as the largest mobile home insurance company, the largest mobile home financing company, and the majority of mobile home dealerships in the United States. And Warren has invested over $20 billion into the mobile home industry.

Mobile Homes and the Increasing Demand for Lower-Cost Housing

Mobile home parks provide a practical low-cost housing solution for those who cannot afford to pay normal rental costs involved in either apartments or traditional single-family homes. There are currently about 75 million people in the U.S. earning less than $25,000 per year. Perhaps half of these individuals can only afford to pay $400 per month (or less) for rent, and mobile home communities provide an affordable housing choice that has many benefits compared to most other low-cost housing alternatives.

Advantages of Mobile Home Parks

Approximately 10 percent of those residing in the United States live in mobile homes. Whether this number increases or not, the rental base is a sizable one. Given economic projections, it is likely that demand will increase while in many areas the supply of mobile home parks is shrinking. Per most studies, mobile homes are not as "mobile" as the name suggests, since about 99 percent of them are still in their original location.

Here are the primary advantages of mobile home park investments:

- Seller financing (all or partial) may be available
- Historically low vacancy rates

- High cost to move mobile homes ($3500 or so) creates tenant stability
- Limited need for capital improvements
- Lowest cost among affordable housing alternatives for renters
- More space and community environment than in low-income apartments
- Land improvements can be depreciated over fifteen years (faster depreciation than apartments)
- Fewer opportunities for something to go wrong with properties
- Buying, selling, and financing mobile homes can provide extra profits
- Expense ratio (30 to 45 percent of gross revenues is common) creates attractive profit potential

For investors who are willing to learn about a specialized form of commercial real estate, mobile home parks can be a rewarding investment opportunity.

Potential Disadvantages of Mobile Home Park Investments

Investors who can successfully manage any potential disadvantages and risks can turn an average investment opportunity into a great one. As with any commercial real estate investment opportunity, smart investors should weigh the potential pros and cons before making a final decision to invest.

Some potential disadvantages of investing in mobile home parks are:

- Limited institutional financing availability
- Specialized insurance requirements
- Shorter economic life of mobile homes compared to traditional "stick built" homes
- Reduced inventory of buying opportunities (less common than apartments)
- Prevailing images of "trailer parks" and lack of familiarity by investors
- Rent is often paid in cash or money orders made out "blank" payee (and may not be included in income)
- Many mobile home parks (other than over-age-fifty-five mobile home parks), receive their income in the form of cash or money orders, which may or may not be deposited into the bank. This can make it difficult to obtain provable financial statements from the current park owners, which in turn makes it difficult to obtain institutional financing

The availability of financing for buying a mobile home park is often more limited because many commercial lenders do not understand this specialized investment category. Seller financing is a common solution to this potential problem, and loan default rates are historically lower than other home loans. It seems likely that the investment participation by Warren Buffett and other savvy investors will improve financial options for both those buying individual mobile homes and commercial real estate investors who want to buy a mobile home community.

Mobile homes depreciate more quickly than traditional homes and apartments, and this accounting and economic factor should be considered when evaluating appraisals, cash flow projections, and length of investments.

Chapter 13

How and Where to Find Commercial Real Estate

If you're looking for a good commercial real estate property to invest in, there are plenty of ways to find one. But there's a difference in finding good property and finding a good deal on property—and to be successful, you need to be able to do both.

If you're looking for investment properties, it's not difficult to find them. The primary source of finding quality commercial real estate will be to look through a combination of resources including:

- Major commercial real estate brokerage firms
- Websites of major commercial brokerage firms
- Commercial real estate websites such as LoopNet.com

If you conduct an internet search, you will come up with an endless stream of companies that offer commercial properties for sale.

The first thing you need to decide is the type of property you'd like to buy. Are you interested in apartments, office, retail, self-storage, or mobile home parks? Whatever your objective, there are several steps you can take to make your search more successful.

Where Do You Find Commercial Real Estate?

Are you curious where to find commercial real estate? First, consider the fact that it's likely to be all around you. Across a city of any size, you'll find restaurants, grocery stores, office buildings, apartment complexes, retail stores, industrial buildings, self-storage units, and many more types of buildings that all fall under the category of commercial real estate. Some of these various storefronts and physical spaces are owned by the company that occupies them, while others are leased by businesses from owners/investors. Generally, commercial real estate professionals will buy properties that they can lease to businesses and other professionals, so if that's your goal, it pays to know the best ways to find a commercial real estate investment worth buying.

Consult with a Commercial Real Estate Broker and/or CCIM

When it comes to finding commercial real estate, it's hard to argue against starting with a commercial real estate broker. You may eventually get to a point where you uncover all of your commercial property deals without outside help from a broker, but if you're still new to the process, a broker's insight and connections can be invaluable. As with any business, there's going to be inside knowledge and information that's not easily accessible. If you're having difficulty finding a broker, start by looking for a good commercial real estate brokerage firm. A CCIM is a certified expert in commercial real estate, who holds a designation as a certified commercial investment member. They are an excellent resource to use to find and evaluate commercial real estate properties. Each CCIM is a licensed real estate broker or agent who specializes in commercial real estate.

Online Search

The internet is a blessing when looking for real estate. On the plus side, it's easier than ever to get a general overview of the local commercial real estate market and see which properties are available. There are some online services that give you a good starting point, but for something as elusive as a great commercial property, you should be prepared to use other search methods. LoopNet.com is an excellent source for buying and selling apartments and other commercial real estate.

Finding Motivated Sellers

Customers are what drive the commercial real estate business. It is important to look for those motivated sellers who may want to sell their property because of retirement, health reasons, etc. and, therefore, willing to sell below market value. If they are not motivated to sell their property, then they will be much less willing to negotiate.

Search Target Areas for Properties

Some investors prefer properties which are within a reasonable distance from their home so they can personally manage it. Others can calculate the prices of a property manager and still turn a profit by purchasing a property in another state. Wherever you decide to look, be sure you can afford multiple in-person visits to the property before buying. Don't ever settle for what pictures and third parties tell you. When looking for a property, you should farm the potential neighborhoods. This means studying the location, seeing other available properties, talking to other neighborhood owners, getting to know the number of commercial building permits being issued in the last few years, learning about the employment rates, and so on.

Talk to Current Owners and Professionals (Find Off-Market Properties)

If you become involved in the local business and commercial real estate community, you will meet people who are in the same game as you. It's essential to make connections with them because there may be an opportunity in the future to work together on a property deal. At the very least, by networking with others, you open yourself to their connections and contacts. If you ever want a deal, you could call some of your contacts and see if they might be interested in selling anything. If they aren't, they very well might know someone who is.

This strategy applies just as well to other professionals connected to commercial property, such as lenders, brokers, title companies, and business owners. By having a network and being immersed in the business community, you stand a greater chance of realizing opportunities that other prospective investors don't have. There's something to be said for having the right of first refusal for great commercial real estate deals.

Keep an Open Mind

Sometimes nothing is more effective than just keeping your eyes peeled for a great deal. That old restaurant you used to eat at might be a great location to own. You might want to consider the new strip malls opening on an affluent side of town. Opportunities present themselves in unexpected places. It's up to you to keep an open mind and be sure to watch for commercial opportunities wherever they appear.

Are there other ways to find commercial real estate? Naturally, the answer is "yes." These are a few of the most common strategies, but one of the things that sets the professional investor apart from the amateur is a willingness to keep innovating and discovering new strategies for uncovering deals. Ultimately, no matter how good you are at crunching the numbers, the only thing that matters is having a deal in front of you that's legitimately worth going for. That's what smart investors work so hard to uncover, day in and day out. One great deal can singlehandedly overtake several mediocre ones in terms of value, and as you get more experience and become more skilled at finding good commercial property, you're likely to see better and better deals coming up.

Do you want to own a commercial property in your local market? That would be the easiest place to manage or oversee. Obviously, if you're starting small with an apartment building, or office, or industrial property, it wouldn't make sense to own a commercial property across the country or even two or three hours from home. If you plan on managing the property yourself—which makes sense if you're starting with a smaller unit—you would be better served to own something in your home market. Owning commercial real estate some distance away can be successfully done with a professional property manager, who is readily available everywhere.

As you expand your commercial real estate business, you may decide to extend your reach to other markets. Staying within the same state or region, however, would make it easier to oversee your properties. While there may be certain areas of the country that are better for commercial real estate investments than others, the fact is there are good properties available in many markets, including yours.

Not every type of commercial real estate property may be a good investment in every area or market. Before you invest in a commercial property, make sure there's a demand for that type of property in the area you're considering. Do research to find out the occupancy rates of properties in the area. If you're interested in apartments, find out how apartments are doing in the area. Are they near capacity or are there high vacancy rates?

It's also important to look at trends. Are occupancy rates in the area increasing or declining? If occupancy rates are climbing, that's a good sign. A rising demand can help ensure that you'll be able fill most of your units. But declining occupancy rates would be a red flag. Declining occupancy rates would mean you'll have trouble filling your units—and may even require you to lower your rent rates to attract tenants.

If the demand in your area is declining, you need to look at investments in other healthier markets. How are lease rates (current rates) doing? Are they rising or declining?

Once you've done your market research and identified a target area, it's time to take a closer look at the properties in that market.

Evaluating Your Options

Once you've decided where you'd like to buy a commercial property, whether it's in your home market or elsewhere—the next step is to zero in on the available properties in that area. Be prepared to be very patient. Talk to several commercial real estate brokers in the area and see what they have to offer. Then, for further evaluation, pick out the properties that make sense to you. You should talk with other local property owners and property managers.

Once you've identified some properties to evaluate, the first step is to do a site evaluation. See what kind of condition the property is in. Does it appear to be in good shape or will it require a major investment to bring it up to acceptable standards.

If you're buying an office, industrial, or retail property, you should take some time to casually talk with some of the tenants and get their input.

NOTE: Refrain from telling the tenants that you are considering buying the property, only that you are interested in how the conditions are. An owner may become angry or irritated if you let tenants know that the building is possibly for sale. ***Ask:*** Are the tenants pleased with the condition of the building or do they have some complaints that would indicate you might need to spend money to fix some lingering problems? Find out if they plan to stick around for a while and renew their leases. If most plan to stay and renew their lease, that's a good sign. If they're planning to move on, you should consider doing the same.

Next, look at other properties in the area to see if they are at or near capacity—and find out what new properties may be under construction or in the planning stages in that market.

It also helps to find a motivated seller. Find a seller who is willing to sell their property at or below the market value. If the seller isn't willing to negotiate, you may need to move on to a seller who is more eager to unload their property at a price that is advantageous to you.

Finally, take a long, in-depth look at the financials. For each property, evaluate the key financials, such as net operating income, capitalization rate, cash flow, and debt service ratio to determine if the property will be a profitable long-term investment for you. If you have several properties that meet your standards, pick the best and make an offer. If not, continue your search until you find a property that works for you. Again, it may take a lot of patience to find a property that is right for you, but there are generally an unlimited number of opportunities in the market, so there is no need to buy a property unless you're convinced it will deliver the results you need to earn the return you require.

Don't panic. We will go into more depth on all the specific financial ratios later in this book.

Chapter 14

How Do You Analyze the Economics of Commercial and Investment Real Estate?

Before you decide where to invest your money in commercial real estate, it's crucial that you understand how to analyze both commercial real estate and the real estate economy, especially as it relates to investing. This means having a firm grasp on the broader economy, as well as the various commercial real estate trends and indicators within your area of interest. Commercial real estate is not directly connected to fluctuations in the residential real estate prices. At the time of writing this edition, commercial real estate is increasing in value. You can be a part of that growth if you know what you're doing.

Commercial real estate has a rich history of serving as a solid intermediate and long-term investment vehicle for professional investors throughout the world. One noteworthy and transformative financial event occurred several decades ago when pension funds and endowments began buying and investing in commercial property, in addition to financing commercial real estate. How did pension fund investment managers decide to invest in commercial real estate? Why do individual, corporate, and retirement investors choose to buy commercial properties today?

While such financial and investing decisions are reached by a unique decision-making process that can differ widely from one case to another, it is likely the analysis will include a satisfactory conclusion about the overall economics of commercial real estate.

Please don't be overwhelmed by the magnitude of all the items in this list of things to analyze about commercial real estate economics. If you gain a general overview of real estate economics, you will be just fine. The portion of an investment feasibility study (from an outside firm that specializes in doing feasibility studies) dealing with commercial real estate economics can be described by a series of straightforward questions (and answers) that include the following areas:

- Supply and demand
- Inflation
- Appreciation potential
- Cash flow
- Valuation and appraisals
- Depreciation and Cost Segregation
- Location
- Tax benefits
- Leverage
- Unemployment
- Economic growth and monetary/fiscal policies
- Risks and risk management
- Availability of commercial real estate loans for construction and permanent financing
- Business potential and marketing
- Number of recent permits for commercial real estate

The general economics involving commercial real estate should examine historical results, current trends, and future projections. Investment analysis of multiple complex factors for the past, present, and future is both challenging and rewarding. Factors like unemployment and economic growth might not vary significantly from one property to another in a specific city or a nearby city, but regional and national differences are common and should be analyzed.

Business Communication and Investment Analysis

When you look at commercial properties as an investment, you must consider the current supply and demand. While that is rudimentary, it is nonetheless imperative. The most ideal property is one that is in an area with a low vacancy rate and limited space for new developments.

A low vacancy rate means few properties in the area are left available to rent on the market for long, thereby increasing the likelihood that your properties will get rented quickly. With limited space for new development, no other properties can be built to satisfy the demand; therefore, the value of existing space increases. Low supply mixed with high demand means you can enjoy higher rental rates.

You must also evaluate the strength of the local economy. This means considering employment rates and economic growth. You must inquire as to the rate at which new commercial building permits are issued. Go back about five years when doing this; it will give you some idea of how the current supply may be affected by any new developments.

The process of analyzing (sometimes conflicting) data and information on commercial real estate projects is ideally facilitated by several expert voices and opinions that might also not agree with each other. This is not the problem that it might appear to be in the first place. Because there are always varying degrees of risk present in any investment activity, it is helpful to have different points of view to keep the potential for managing those possible risks in an appropriate perspective.

When deciding whether to invest, it will not always be practical to have a unanimous decision that points in one obvious direction or the other. Some of the factors noted in the list above might be diametrically opposed to each other, and a team of financial experts might totally disagree about what the numbers are indicating. Some economic data is subject to individual interpretation, while other results are produced by an impersonal formula that never varies. The group dynamics can have an influence on the investment decision, and the effectiveness of business communication and collaboration can also play a role in the outcome of the overall analysis. You need to sort and sift the data and recommendations from others and come to your own conclusions.

Are Some Economic Factors More Important Than Others for Commercial Real Estate?

You're ultimately responsible for the knowledge you bring to any investing deal. That's why it pays to uncover the information relevant to the commercial real estate market. One step is to channel your inner-city planner or developer, and find out everything you can about the future of the city you've chosen.

The kinds of information you want include zoning, property usage, planning regulations, future growth prospects, potential new businesses and employers moving in, and more. This will tell you where businesses are likely to settle and suggest which direction property prices are going to move. Your local Chamber of Commerce is often able to help you with this economic data and analysis. Additionally, there are dozens of economic and business data resources online. Subscribe to and regularly read the ***Local Journal of Business*** to gain a better insight into the local market.

Another important factor to consider is the history of commercial real estate sales in your area. What trends do you see in the prices of properties in the last three years? Trends will have a big impact on the viability of the investments you're considering. When it comes to commercial real estate, you can't be afraid to get in there and do some hands-on work. Whether it's talking to people in the community or inspecting a lot of properties, there's a lot you can do to determine the strength of a local economy for commercial property.

It's also important to note that researching commercial property is an ongoing process, particularly for someone who's hoping to become or who already is a commercial real estate investor. Other great ways to get insight into the local economy is to monitor advertisements for commercial property sales and leases, and talking to lenders or banks that deal with commercial real estate. While it might take some time to get the kind of results you want, you're sure to benefit from conducting your own research and diving headfirst into learning about the area where you're going to invest. Talk with local commercial real estate brokers, CCIMs, or a commercial real estate mentor. You could and should also search online on major commercial brokerage firm's websites and on websites like LoopNet.com.

Cash flow can frequently involve significant opportunities to improve. The absence of positive cash flow as reflected in current accounting statements does not prevent future improvements. Operating expenses can often be reduced in conjunction with increasing gross income from sales or tenant leases that result in an increase of Net Operating Income (NOI).

Business potential and marketing is an area that can make an average investment into an exceptional one. This explains an attraction by professional investors to a distressed or turnaround real estate project. With skilled managers, a money-losing venture can be transformed into a profitable investment. This is, however, challenging and requires a combination of patience, hard work, flexibility, and a Plan-B mentality to make it workable on a regular basis.

Evolution of Property Prices

Commercial and residential real estate have different economic characteristics generated by varying factors. Commercial buildings are multifamily residential buildings, office spaces, warehouses, industrial complexes, shopping centers, hospitals, hotels, etc. A clear distinction is made by the industries of construction, loans, brokerage and investment, and the market participants must have specialized training to be able to address this market.

In the last thirty-five years, commercial and residential property prices have evolved independently, as commercial real estate buyers have different capital sources. The capital invested in the commercial real estate market has evolved and diversified to include public and private sources of capital.

Private investors and syndicates have become an important role in capital markets, the commercial real estate market is no longer dependent on them. Beginning in 2005, groups of more sophisticated and better capitalized buyers were responsible for 50 to 60 percent of the purchases of commercial properties. These sources of capital flows have fundamentally changed the nature of the commercial real estate market since 1980 and the diversity and availability of capital made it far less volatile.

TSIC (Title Secured Mortgages)

Commercial mortgage securitization introduced public capital in commercial real estate markets. The titles for securitized commercial mortgages (TSIC) were introduced by a government resolution in 1990 and are the largest generators of commercial mortgages. At the time of this book's writing, the amounts generated by TSIC reached $170 billion, an increase of about 8.5 times in the last decade. Internationally, TSIC experienced a doubling of capital invested in commercial real estate. The introduction of interstate banking activities allowed commercial banks to more easily transfer capital between countries.

Many international banks have invested in the commercial real estate market in the recent past and their investments have increased.

In the U.S., the volume of investments in commercial buildings doubled between 2009 and 2010, rising from $14 billion in 2009 to $31 billion in 2010. This sharp rise led to domestic and inter-regional activity in the U.S., with investors and foreign buyers who have invested in these markets in commercial real estate.

The biggest change that has occurred in the commercial real estate market since the early eighties is the way it is perceived by the investors. With the public sector's increasing involvement, the level of information and research in the field has improved dramatically.

The commercial real estate market has seen a significant development in its dimensions, becoming open to international investors, which led to a dramatic improvement of liquidity in this market. The influence of commercial real estate market globalization is highlighted in the important role it plays globally. Fortunately, individual commercial real estate investors are still a dominate force in the commercial real estate arena, especially for properties that are under $2 million.

What Role Does Plan B Have in Real Estate Economics?

While some might wonder what role Plan B has in this overview, the use of economics is not an exact science, whether applied to commercial real estate or to any other part of a changing economy. Inflation is just one illustration. How much inflation will we have during the next five to ten years and when will it happen? Who can be sure how inflationary the economy will be? Much like the weather, economies have a way of suddenly taking unexpected twists and turns.

Plan-B thinking is a thoughtful and smart way of looking ahead and anticipating what to do when and if the unexpected happens. While this might represent the part of economics that many investors overlook, the most successful investment professionals are always thinking several steps ahead.

They are constantly concentrating on what to do if something goes wrong or if property value starts going up dramatically. Such contingency planning is often guided by asking questions about different scenarios, choices, and opportunities.

One Question Leads to Another

Asking the right questions about economic analysis for property investing will often lead to other vital questions of interest. Building upon the information above, one of the right questions should examine the financial benefits of an all-cash investment in comparison to a leveraged acquisition. Another suggested area of inquiry is to analyze the possible risks and opportunities involving cash flow projections. Some of the reasons for cash flow shortfalls or cash flow increases can relate to economics or correct property management.

Given the positive change in commercial mortgage financing for some types of properties, detailed questions should be asked about what variations of business financing are available and which are not. How much of this depends on the economy? The questions and answers about pricing and availability of commercial property loans should also be part of the conversation about the use of cash instead of debt to make a timely purchase.

Talk to Other or Current Commercial Property Owners

It might seem counterintuitive to talk to people who might very well be your competition, but when you're just starting out, it can be a viable strategy. While consulting with agents and brokers is the choice most people think of, it's very likely that actual owners are the better experts in the areas where they own commercial property. They're the ones immersed in the business and have ties to other business owners in the community. By the time you own commercial property, you will need to be just as knowledgeable about your chosen location. These other commercial property owners may be willing to sell their properties with partial and/or up to 100 percent seller financing.

Consult with Commercial Agents or Brokers

While it's not necessarily a requirement for you to work with a commercial brokerage firm, you are likely to benefit from the experience of working with one while you're still new to commercial real estate investing. If you can't find any other owners who want to sell their property in the area, a broker is the best source of timely and accurate information about the economies of commercial real estate in the area and properties available to purchase.

It's the job of industry professionals to maintain extensive knowledge about the economy and market trends, making a good commercial agent or broker an important resource for your efforts. Additionally, CCIMs (Certified Commercial Investment Members) are a great resource.

In fact, Chapter 20 of this book provides a comprehensive discussion and description of the value and services that a CCIM can provide for commercial real estate investors.

Investing with Knowledge Is Smart and Can Be Profitable

One other interesting point is the fact that areas without much financial or economic data might just be places to avoid. If you're spending a lot of your time and energy trying to uncover important data points, and you're not making any progress, it might be best to move on to a new area. The last thing you want to do is blindly invest in a property without first understanding the area, and then having a solid analysis of the property itself. You can also consider looking to market research firms to provide you with up-to-date insights and data about the trends and conditions of commercial real estate. The local Chamber of Commerce and other local sources may present a rosier spin of current local data. The National Association of Realtors and the state and local Board of Realtors' websites provide recent data to the public, free of charge. Most major commercial brokerage firms regularly issue reports on the various types of commercial real estate, such as reports on the office market, retail, and housing as well as the data across the country, broken down into specific local areas.

Ultimately, it's a combination of these and other strategies that will give you a comprehensive understanding of the local commercial real estate market. The more you know, the better you'll be able to make wise investing decisions and a success out of your commercial real estate investing career.

The overall goal to be accomplished by analyzing commercial real estate economics is to help make a better-informed, intelligent investment decision. When done effectively, it is part of a successful strategy for making smart investing choices.

Commercial real estate investment is great for individuals with a basic or advanced knowledge about the subject. Before you invest, you should make sure you have the time and money needed to manage your commercial real estate or hire a property manager to oversee your property.

While the above is a good overview to start with when investing in commercial real estate, the focus must always be on the specific property first. Examine the historic financial performance—the strength and quality of the property leases and income. And, as always, do the entire in-depth due diligence process.

Most importantly, get all the actual financial data, such as the income, expenses, and the actual historical current occupancy data for the last three years, on any potential commercial property upfront.

Fall in love with the numbers, not the building, its projections, or its hype.

Chapter 15

Marketing Analysis on the Target Commercial Property

When considering a target commercial property, it is important to analyze the market. This is true for every type of commercial property including office buildings, apartments, retail properties, mobile home parks, and self-storage units.

When you complete your market analysis of a commercial property, there are eight main parts:

1. Gather data and conduct a specific market analysis and competitive analysis
2. Gather data and conduct political, demographic, and legal analyses
3. Gather data and conduct property location and site analyses
4. Gather and analyze the actual (real) property financial data (the data should include the last three years' Actuals and be compared to the seller/broker's prepared Pro Forma)
5. Gather and analyze the local, national, and world economies
6. Analyze technology and lifestyle of the area
7. Gather the data and analyze the current demand versus the current inventory of that type of commercial property

8. Get and analyze 1) the actual historical occupancy and 2) the detailed current occupancy data

Competition mapping provides a guide of the competitors to a selected property. As an example, a retailer who intends to open a new location should take the competitors' data into consideration before doing so to determine if there are too many similar businesses in the same area. If there are, then he or she might opt for an area with fewer competitors.

The competitor analysis includes aspects such as:

- Identification of who the competition is
- The location of the competition
- The products they are selling?
- What the competing properties are renting for and what percentage of their building is currently leased

This can also be done with a gap analysis, which represents a report compiled from the competitors' data and market information on a certain location to determine if there are any gaps for the products they are selling. To do so, this takes into consideration the market, the information available on the location, the residents' lifestyles and shopping habits, the workforce available, demographic aspects, data on the competitors, and market gaps.

The **PEST** analysis is also useful for finding the market's growth or decline. "**PEST**" stands for Political, Economic, Social, and Technological factors. These are factors which are used to assess the market for a business or organizational unit.

Political:

The political aspects include ecological/environmental issues, as well as current and future legislation. It also includes international legislation, regulatory bodies and processes, and government policies. Things such as terms and changes, grants and initiatives, trading policies, funding, home market lobbying, and pressure groups are also included. One should take into consideration international pressure groups, wars, and conflicts.

Economic:

The economic aspects include home economy situation and trends, seasonality, market and trade cycles, taxation specific to product/services, market routes and distribution trends, customer/end-user drivers, specific industry factors, overseas economies and trends, general taxation issues, interest and exchange rates, and international trade or monetary issues.

Social:

The social point of view concerns things such as the different demographics and lifestyle trends, the media views, and consumer attitudes. It also includes the brands, consumer buying patterns, law changes that affect social factors, technological image, major events, ethnic and religious factors, as well as fashion and role models and buying trends.

Technological:

The technological aspects include competing technology development, as well as replacement technology/solutions, research funding, information and communications, and technology legislation. It further consists of innovation potential manufacturing maturity and capacity, associated/dependent technologies, the maturity of technology, information and communications, as well as licensing, patents, technology access, consumer buying mechanisms/technology, and advertising and publicity, and ethical issues.

Commercial property valuation is determined mainly by two factors: the current Net Operating Income and the Cap Rate.

Along with the economic and demographic changes, the commercial real estate industry also showed some shifting in its assumptions. Speaking on a panel at the Strategic Real Estate Conference in New York, economists agreed that this is a time of incredible change, but that they also see opportunity. If before, the office space was from 500 to 700 square feet per person, nowadays, the average office allows 200 square feet per person. Also, a very important change was produced once the technology started to develop in the computer era.

The real estate market is determined by the relationship between supply and demand; the relation between these two being calculated as “available inventory.” So, at the current sales prices, how long would it take to sell the total number of properties available on the market? The inventory is measured in weeks and months, and longer inventory periods are associated with buyers’ markets, while shorter inventory periods are associated with sellers’ markets. There are buyers and sellers who try to time their purchase to take advantage of market cycles.

Chapter 16

Key Financial Ratios for Evaluating Income Properties

Per the leading management guru of the twentieth century and well-known bestselling author on management, Dr. Peter Drucker, "What gets measured—gets managed." That thought in mind, it is imperative you treat any investment as you would a personal company and give it the best in management. "Manage your commercial real estate by the numbers."

In the commercial real estate business, there are some key financial ratios that should be known by every buyer, owner, manager, and agent. It is these numbers that help you manage your property. You need to "fall in love with the numbers—not just the property." But more than that, you need to know how each number is to be calculated.

While there are many factors that go into determining the true value of an income property, commercial real estate investors rely on several key formulas to come up with a general idea of the potential value of a property and the return on investment they could reasonably expect if they were to purchase the property.

We start off with this, what we call "scheduled income." What's that? Say you have a 10-unit apartment and the scheduled rent for each one is $400 a month, but they're not all occupied. Let's say only nine are occupied and the tenant of one of them is slow paying. So how do we deal with that? We deduct that from the income. We don't count what isn't there. Next, that slow pay is a collection loss for right now and hopefully we get it back on track, but currently, you're not getting it. You only count income you have actually received. That's straight forward. You need to know how much you have coming in.

Now from that, we deduct the actual operating expenses, which are the following:

1. Utilities
2. Property taxes (both real and personal property)
3. Insurance
4. Maintenance and repairs
5. Property management

Now there could be some miscellaneous fees like legal, accounting, marketing, and other items to account for as well.

We take all these operating expenses, total them, and subtract that number from the actual income. The result is the NOI—the net operating income. That's what NOI is, nothing more and nothing less.

Many times, what's important for you to look for when you're looking at a listing is that some of these expenses may be a little off or missing entirely. How could that be? It's simple; they take off the property management and they don't include it. It's not there. They're just assuming you're going to manage it yourself. Well, holy mackerel, that was 10 percent or more of the expenses! Now is that legitimate? Is that legal? Yeah, but guess what? They're assuming you're going to manage it yourself, so they accidentally, on purpose, deducted something that uses about 10 percent of all the expenses. Watch for it.

Sometime what they do not include is critical.

How about maintenance and repairs? The question is, is it high, low, or missing? If they tell you they have a lot of expenses for repairs and maintenance, you must be concerned about that. If you have a low number, you also need to be concerned about that because maybe they did a lot of the work last year and now this year the building doesn't need it. And watch out, because if they did major remodeling, the remodeling is not maintenance and repair. It will never show up because it is a capital expenditure that capitalized and depreciated over time. Those are some hints of what to look for. And lastly, if it's missing completely, that's a red flag. You cannot have no repairs. That could be 20 to 40 percent of the operating expenses, so it can't be zero. However, there may be tenants' reimbursements in office and retail properties, which is awesome.

I hope you understand NOI because it's a foundational piece for you. When you're looking at a financial statement you need to see what the numbers tell you. This one thing separates you from getting a deal or not getting a deal.

Drill down, get those numbers. And get the actual financials (actual income and operating expenses) for the last three years of operation. Don't accept anything less. Also, get the last three years' rent rolls and the detailed current rent roll, which includes the individual unit's square footage, rent, renewal options and rate, other items like parking or storage fees, the name of the individual or company in the unit, and information on any triple net reimbursements, percentage leases in retail, such as triple net leases, for office or retail.

Actual Net operating income is critical. It's critical for you to understand how much money this property is making, which will tell you how much money you have left over after paying your expenses to pay your loan payment. The lender has the same question: Is there enough money left over to pay them? That's why NOI is so important to understand.

And the NOI is used to construct the capitalization rate or what we call "cap rate." Now what the heck is cap rate? Cap rate is nothing more or less than the net income as a percentage of the valuation.

It's the value of the property. It's a formula. It's a division problem from elementary school. So, let's just do it this way: take the NOI of a subject property of the $100,000. That's a nice number. Let's say that the listing price is $900,000. We divide $900,000 into $100,000 and we get 0.111. Easy. But what does that number tell us? It is equivalent to 11.1 percent, all we do is take off the percent sign and call it cap rate, in this case, an 11.1 cap rate. In other words, the property provides an 11.1 percent return. Higher is better for the buyer and lower is better for a seller.

It's a simple equation: NOI divided by the value. Now I say we're doing multiple values and multiple cap rates. Why? Because I don't pay retail. I don't want you to pay retail, is that ok with you? We're going to take the $100,000, but we only want to pay $800,000. We just got a new division problem, don't we? Basically, that becomes 0.125 or 12.5 %, which we call a 12.5 Cap Rate. I'd like to buy in at a higher cap rate; wouldn't you? Do your due diligence and ensure the numbers are accurate. If the cap rate is too high (such as 15) and seems unbelievable, it most likely is not real and just a high projection.

Why is cap rate so important? And how does that affect things? Because you get a higher return on your money. A higher cap rate for you as a buyer means you have greater return and you're getting greater value because you're buying it for less and getting the same amount of income. A 9 or 10 cap rate is stellar. If you've got more than single digits, you've got a killer potential property. If it gets too high though, you must say "Huh?" If it looks too good to be true, maybe it is.

Here are several of the most common—and most critical—financial ratios used in the commercial real estate business.

Net Operating Income (NOI)

One of the most important pieces of information you will need to know in evaluating the value of a property is the "net operating income." The NOI tells you how much income you would likely be earning on this property after accounting for all your expenses.

You can calculate NOI (which is potential rental income minus vacancies, and credit losses) by using the following formula:

NOI = ACTUAL INCOME - ACTUAL OPERATING EXPENSES

[Note: Debt Service is not an operating expense and is not used in calculating NOI.]

Vacancy Rate/Occupancy Rate

One of the most important numbers is the current and actual (not proforma) vacancy rate, which shows the number of available units divided by the total number of units available for rent on a property. The vacancy rate should be as low as possible. Vacancy rate is calculated using the following formula, and the result is a percentage:

VACANCY RATE = TOTAL NUMBER OF UNOCCUPIED UNITS IN A PROPERTY ÷ TOTAL NUMBER OF UNITS IN A PROPERTY

In exchange, the occupancy rate is determined by subtracting the vacancy rate from 100 percent. The formula is as follows:

OCCUPANCY RATE = 100% – VACANCY RATE

Depreciation Rate

The depreciation rate determines the amount of the property's value that was lost over time, because of the age and conditions. The depreciation rate is an expense. Depreciation is completed over a 27.5-year period and applies only to the (residential) apartment building, but not to the land included in the property.

The depreciation term for non-residential commercial real estate is 39 years (excluding the land.) The formula for calculating depreciation starts with the building's value:

BUILDING VALUE = PURCHASE PRICE – LAND VALUE

After calculating the building value, we can calculate the depreciations, based on the type of property:

ANNUAL DEPRECIATION = APARTMENT BUILDING VALUE ÷ 27.5 YEARS

ANNUAL DEPRECIATION = COMMERCIAL BUILDING VALUE ÷ 39 YEARS

Capitalization Rate (Cap Rate)

Once you know the NOI, you can calculate the cap rate to see how the value of a commercial property relates to its future income. You would calculate the cap rate using the following:

CAP RATE = NET OPERATING INCOME (NOI) ÷ BY PRICE* OR PROPERTY VALUE

*Price could be: a) Listing Price, b) Offer Price, or c) Accepted Offer Price. Do each calculation separately as needed.

For example, if you purchased a property for $400,000 that has net operating income of $40,000 a year, your cap rate would be 10 ($40,000 ÷ $400,000 = 10%)—a 10 Cap.

The higher the price (relative to the NOI), the lower the cap rate. For instance, if the price is $500,000, the cap rate would be 8 ($40,000 ÷ $500,000 = 8%). On the other hand, if the price was $300,000, the cap rate would be 13.33 ($40,000 ÷ $300,000 = 13.33%).

Chapter 17

Contracts to Purchase Commercial Real Estate with or without a Broker

Have you found a promising commercial property at a fair price that you're reasonably confident will make you money? If the cash flow seems good and the overall value seems to be a bargain, then you're ready to finally take the plunge and purchase a piece of commercial real estate. Of course, now should begin the actual purchase process. Assuming you've done your full entire due diligence and chosen a good property, you should prepare a contract and secure financing to bring the whole deal to a close. Usually, you'll work with a team of people, including an accountant, real estate attorney, commercial mortgage broker, and often your commercial real estate broker.

The process of buying commercial real estate will eventually result in preparing and submitting a contract to purchase a specific commercial property. This is a legal document that begins the contractual process leading to the title changing hands from the current owner to you. Before reaching this key milestone on your way to a commercial real estate acquisition, it is advisable to consider what expert help you want or need to complete your purchase.

A decision about including or excluding a commercial real estate broker is likely to happen at an early point in the search process for suitable property acquisition candidates. Under many circumstances, a broker would probably be relied upon to identify some or all the properties to be included in the analysis of ideal purchase opportunities.

How Do You Prepare a Contract to Purchase Commercial Real Estate, both with and without a Commercial Real Estate Broker?

Preparing your commercial real estate purchase agreement might seem daunting at first, but once it is signed, it will embody your entire agreement. When you begin either with or without a commercial broker, it is imperative that you remember which side of the transaction is your side, and the bargaining strength you have. The negotiation process will seem simpler with a broker on your side to offer aid, but the main points remain the same in your agreement—with or without a broker. If the commercial property is listed with a commercial broker, then you will be preparing and submitting your contract to buy with that broker or agent.

The seller and the broker will usually want to bind the buyer into a contract, without having to provide extensive warranties or representations. In contrast, the purchaser will want a longer review time to ensure the environmental, physical, and legal condition of the property before being bound by an agreement. Neither side will get exactly what they want but the purchase agreement can tip the scale to one side or another. This is a give and take, negotiated package of price, terms, financing, warranties, and representations.

If you are the purchaser, you want to make sure that you have adequate opportunity to inspect the property without any interference. You will also want time to complete your entire full due diligence and for the title company, your real estate attorney, and you to review the title. During the completion of the entire full diligence process, should you find a problem with the commercial property, your transaction can be terminated, and you can receive a full refund of all deposits or earnest monies, as long as those terms are stipulated with a time limit in your contract, and that you have not exceeded that time frame.

If the property is in a market that is rapidly developing, or there are many interested buyers, you may prepare the initial draft that has minimal warranties from the seller, short due diligence, and a larger money deposit that goes to the purchaser immediately after the execution of the agreement.

This brings us to a logical question: What are some reasons that a commercial real estate buyer might choose to exclude a broker from their contract and offer process? You decide.

Preparing a Contract to Purchase with a Commercial Real Estate Broker

Experienced commercial real estate investors may choose to handle the purchase process on their own. But anyone who's relatively new to the game will probably benefit greatly from a licensed commercial real estate broker. One of the main reasons for this is because a commercial broker is highly knowledgeable and can help you with the things you don't even know that you don't know. In other words, they're there to help keep you from overlooking anything that would be catastrophic for your finances. On the other side of the equation, their connections and experience in negotiation can yield you more favorable terms.

Real estate sales professionals are sometimes criticized for the large commissions involved in what they do. They do not work for free. What is expert real estate advice worth to you?

The seller (not the buyer) is responsible for paying the sales commission to both the listing and selling brokers. Buyers effectively get the services of a commercial real estate broker for nothing. That sounds like a pretty good deal to most purchasers looking for a cost-effective transaction. Some brokers also offer a specialized fee arrangement in which they represent the buyer rather than the seller; in this case, a buyer may pay a designated fee for "buyer's agreement" services. It is a reasonable compromise to deal with concerns about brokers representing sellers more than buyers. Do you think there might be a possible conflict of focus since the higher the price, the more the selling and listing brokers earn?

Note: Unlisted commercial property deals can be done directly with the owner, without a broker.

When it comes time to purchase a property through a commercial real estate broker, you and the broker should first negotiate and craft a purchase agreement with the seller. This is the area where it's so helpful to have a broker, because it's his or her job to understand these complex contracts and tailor the agreement in a transaction to the realities of that situation. You'll need to work with the owner and maybe with your broker to hammer out acceptable terms.

Make sure the other party is truly the owner of the property (always verify property's title with a Title Company) and in a proper position to accept a purchase. Then, discuss carefully with your broker how much time you'll need to close. That means including contingent conditions like gathering and reviewing all the financial information, leases, zoning requirements, as well as securing financing, and much more.

One of the reasons buyers might think of working with a commercial real estate broker and a local real estate attorney is to obtain both business and legal advice. There are several stages during this investment process in which investors should seek legal opinions and guidance from one or more real estate attorneys. The presence of a broker is not designed to replace the separate practical need for the advice and counsel of a trusted real estate lawyer.

Here are a few illustrations of why real estate buyers might choose to include a commercial real estate broker as they move forward to a successful culmination of their contract to purchase a commercial property:

- Professional help in property selection
- Localized expertise about zoning, politics, businesses, and personalities (such as builders and owners)
- Help with confidentiality concerns from someone who understands local problem areas
- Specialized and expert help (even lawyers and physicians need help from other attorneys and doctors)
- Unique negotiating skills
- Ability to successfully handle a potential conflict of interest
- Preference for a collaborative approach to investing
- A "second opinion" about a significant investment

Investors and buyers should think about their own preferences when assembling a personal list of pros and cons of using commercial real estate brokers. The goal here is to facilitate a thoughtful approach for a timely decision about going one direction or the other at an early stage in the investment process.

Possible Reasons for Proceeding without a Commercial Real Estate Broker

The choice to buy an unlisted commercial property without the help of a commercial real estate broker can include reasons such as the following:

- Plan to negotiate directly with an owner of an unlisted property
- Personal background as an attorney or an experienced commercial real estate investor
- Help in selecting properties is not needed
- Highest level of confidentiality is necessary
- Have not identified an acceptable broker to help
- Perception that brokers are primarily working for the sellers paying a commission (Possible conflict of focus as both the listing and selling real estate agents have a fiduciary responsibility to the seller)
- Desire to deal directly with builders or owners of commercial properties before they are listed
- Potential conflicts of interest (especially in smaller markets)

The commercial property is not listed, so the broker will not be paid by the seller and may not want to work without a promise of commission or fees.

These are some considerations that might cause commercial real estate buyers to begin a purchase process without a broker to help represent their interests. It should be noted that most of the examples shown are based on buyer perceptions as to how the commercial property acquisition process works.

Depending on circumstances, the reality of dealing with a commercial real estate broker might not match the initial buyer's perceptions. In other words, perceived problem areas such as those described above might involve incorrect assumptions about what brokers do or don't do.

National restaurant chains and major retail companies, such as Walmart, often desire total secrecy when they start examining the possibility of establishing their initial presence in an area. In some cases, this means they may not or may not want any involvement with local brokers who they do not know or trust. However, in several real-life examples, these serious and smart buyers have chosen to trust one or more local commercial real estate brokers because of their practical conclusion that the benefits outweigh any potential risks or costs of doing so. A significant element in determining potential value for real estate is "location." A thorough understanding of this factor often benefits from the specialized knowledge of a local real estate expert.

In the list above, the most serious and valid reason for excluding a broker is the inability to find one that you like and trust. This might require creativity such as working with other real estate experts, including local commercial real estate owners, architects, and construction companies, until the right person can be identified. Selecting a trustworthy advisor can take time and effort.

If you do not require a "local" expert, then your choice of a commercial real estate broker can be made from other locations where you might find (or already have) a more comfortable fit.

Preparing a Contract without a Broker

If you've decided to forego a broker and you have the expertise to do it yourself, it's still highly recommended that you engage the services of a good local commercial real estate attorney. The impetus here is that someone besides you with real estate experience should look over the contract to make sure that it'll do its job correctly. You might work with an attorney instead of a broker and just pay the hourly fee, which is still substantially less than a large percent commission of the sale price. Usually the sale's commission is paid to the broker by the seller. If you choose to do it all on your own, be sure to avoid the tempting mistake of using a boilerplate agreement that doesn't consider the nuances of your current transaction.

As for the contract itself, you'll need to include a purchase price and the terms of the agreement. Be extra vigilant in situations where you're purchasing from an entity like a business, such as an LLC or corporation, where the sales and purchase agreement requires the signatures of more than one person to be valid. This could also include a vote of the shareholders if the business in question is a corporation. Include the legal description and physical address of the premises, the deed to be transferred, and any additional property that's included in the transaction, such as furniture or vehicles.

Finally, put in any reasonable and necessary contingencies as a buyer that will enable you to back out with a refund of your deposits and/or earnest money in full if something goes wrong. Most buyers require time to secure financing from a lender—you can cancel the contract with no liability if you can't obtain the money within an agreed-upon time frame. Add your entire document requests, the closing date, title company, escrow office, and any adjustments that might be made at closing.

This is a general overview of what it takes to prepare a contract, but it's always a good idea to get more information from a professional real estate legal advisor, especially when you're ready to purchase a commercial property. This sensitive information should remain confidential whether the transaction closes or not.

Confidentiality

Be sure to include confidentiality provisions to protect both parties if the agreement fails, as sensitive information is often shared during negotiations.

Deposits

The earnest money deposit acts as a consideration for entering the purchase contract. It also offers incentive for the commercial real estate broker and seller to work with the purchaser to conduct due diligence quickly. Lastly, it can be liquidated damages if there is a breach of contract. An earnest money deposit is one that is delivered to escrow or the closing attorney upon entering the purchasing agreement, not deposited with the broker or the seller. There should be a separate third-party escrow agreement. When you draft your agreement, you should determine who is responsible for holding the deposit in escrow. Neither the seller nor the broker should hold the deposit.

You should also state the terms of the deposit—when it will be delivered to escrow or the closing attorney, never to the seller or his or her broker. If you are using an escrow agent or closing attorney, you will want to spell out the duties and obligations for the agent, and maybe include a hold harmless and indemnity provision.

Standard practice is for the deposit to be deemed "nonrefundable" but only after the expiration period of a full and entire due diligence. While the deposit may become nonrefundable, it does not mean it is released to the seller prior to closing or after a deal collapse (failure). You can, of course, insert a clause that allows the purchaser to extend their period of due diligence in exchange for an additional deposit, or without any additional deposit by the buyer.

Entire Full Due Diligence Process Time

This is the period the purchaser should inspect the property, do all verifications, and complete the entire full due diligence process. Generally, they are given at least thirty days to several months. When you draft your agreement, you must be clear as to what constitutes the "trigger" of the due diligence period, or what starts it and when it ends. The trigger may be the receipt of survey and commitment for title insurance. You may include an environmental review period, which is triggered by the receipt of an environmental property assessment. Receipt and review of all leases, financials, zoning and entitlement documents, and inspections need to be revealed in addition to the other items. The entire full due diligence process includes everything you need to ensure that the property and its financials are as they were presented.

During the due diligence process and prior to the end of the due diligence period, other concerns may be raised. You should include a time frame that the seller must cure any objections raised by the purchaser. If the objections are not cured, you can include the option of terminating the agreement in exchange for a complete refund or waiving any objections and closing the agreement. If the deal fails, you should have a provision to refund all your deposits and/or earnest monies.

Representations and Warranties

The longer period of due diligence a purchaser gets, does not necessarily reduce warranties and representations the seller will give. The opposite is also true. The shorter the period for due diligence, the more warranties and representations the seller will give.

Therefore, when you draft a purchasing agreement, you not only want to ensure that the seller has all authority to enter the transaction, but that there are:

- No unrecorded liens against the property
- No pending judgments or litigation against the seller or the property
- No outstanding leases or options to lease other than those delivered to the buyer of the property
- No other parties with rights or interest in the subject commercial property
- No violations of laws and ordinances (current, past, or pending)
- No environmental contamination on the property
- No current or prospective title or zoning title
- No recorded judgment against the seller or the property

Finally, you want to ensure that all information given by the seller to the purchaser is true and accurate. Some of these matters may overlap with aspects of the title insurance, but so be it. It is in the best interest of the purchaser to have an agreement drafted in conjunction with the title insurance policy. This is because title insurance policies will not necessarily cover things such as environmental matters.

Remedies

Remedies are a heavily negotiated section. If the seller breaches contract, the purchaser will want entitlement to remedies. Since the purchase agreement is in and of itself a mutually agreed upon transaction, it is important that remedies be noted. If the purchaser breaches the contract, the seller typically gets a remedy related to the deposit—therefore the deposit should be large enough to compensate the seller for the time that the property spent off the market, and it should also be large enough to deter any insincere purchaser.

Overall, when you are preparing a commercial real estate purchase agreement, you need to clarify and negotiate the terms specifically. It is this attention to detail that will ensure agreeable terms.

It is critical to have a knowledgeable commercial real estate attorney draft (or at least review) your entire purchase contract.

Why Work on Your Own?

This is realistic when you are directly dealing with a commercial real estate property owner. Without a broker, you're essentially accepting all the duties and responsibilities a commercial real estate broker performs. Aside from the money you might save the seller on an unlisted property, there could be some other benefits to doing the process on your own. Some people find that brokers are too apt to focus on selling their own listings and they have a relationship with the sellers. This may create a conflict of focus (and perhaps a contractual conflict of interest).

Another possible reason to skip the broker is because they can potentially get in the way of a deal. If you are depending on someone to handle aspects of a transaction, such as the contract, and they're not doing a reliable and forthright job, you might find it more efficient to handle these concerns on your own.

If the property is listed, you will use a commercial real estate broker. Some sellers do not list because they don't want to pay a broker's commission and therefore may be willing to reduce the purchase price if you deal with them directly. In this case, you should have your entire team in place, including a commercial real estate attorney, title company, escrow company, inspection team, commercial mortgage brokers, and others, as needed.

Chapter 18

What Resources Can a Title Company Provide Investors?

You might be surprised to learn that a title company is one of the best sources of information to help you find and analyze commercial real estate, including apartments. A title company's job is to facilitate a successful transaction among all parties involved, including buyers, sellers, escrow offices, mortgage lenders, and real estate agents. Title company escrow reviews the sales contract and goes through the title process to ensure the title is clear, the property taxes are paid, and loan documents are in order, as well as other important tasks.

Successful commercial real estate investment involves a delicate balance of evaluating, selecting, negotiating, buying, managing, and selling properties—such as apartments and office buildings. Without proper planning and help, unexpected legal and financial risks can be introduced into the process. Commercial property investors should seek expert professional help during each stage to protect their assets and to verify the facts and realities of the commercial property.

Real estate title companies are an important source of expert help throughout several stages of the commercial real estate acquisition process. Because a title company can be instrumental in facilitating the transfer of title from the seller to the buyer, each investor should realize what resources title companies can provide to help them.

The Importance of a Good Title Company

The title company is an integral part of any commercial real estate professional's team. Having a close relationship with your title company can make a huge difference in how successful your real estate efforts are. A close relationship means that the title company is easy to reach for quick consultations on vital issues, but at the same time, you want the company to be efficient and experienced in commercial real estate.

It's nearly impossible to successfully purchase a commercial property without effectively using a good title company, which is why you should take your time and interview various prospective title companies before you make a decision.

Analyzing Titles and Other Documents

It might seem obvious, but one of the most essential functions of a title company is to determine the history of a property's title through the title abstract. This is a crucial analysis because without it, you run the risk of purchasing a property to which you don't have free and clear ownership. Along with the title, your title company can provide you with verification that a commercial property's taxes are adequately paid, that the homeowner's association and utility bills are all paid, that there are no undisclosed outstanding loans to pay off, and more. If the title company sees any problems, they will report them and give you a chance to evaluate your options, including the opportunity to back out of a bad deal.

Selecting a Title Company to Acquire Commercial Property

Title companies are not pre-determined or assigned randomly. A commercial real estate investor is likely to choose which company will fill this role for completing his or her purchase. It is advisable to select a title company that has an established reputation for providing timely, thorough, and cost-effective commercial title and escrow real estate services.

A title company is an important part of the professional team used by commercial property investors. This team of real estate experts is likely to include a commercial real estate broker and attorney (among others). These advisors will typically have prior experiences and working relationships that can make the choice of a title company for an investor more fully-informed.

It is also possible that some investor resources, such as property profiles, can be obtained in an expedited manner through a title company during the early stages of the acquisition process. For specialized transactions, such as a 1031 tax-deferred exchange, it will be especially advisable to have significant early communication with one or more prospective title companies or escrow offices regarding their abilities to handle any unique requirements. With exchanges involving commercial properties, such as apartments in two different states, there can be special legal circumstances that need to be taken into consideration when making a title company selection.

There's a wide range of other common resources available at a title company. These resources can help you to find and analyze commercial real estate.

Most title company's websites feature tools and resources that can point you in the direction you need to go. This might include databases and maps for locating available properties and a title fee calculator. These tools make it easier to determine, based on your unique situation, whether a property is worth the investment.

Primary Examples of Title Company Resources for Commercial Investing

Several examples of services typically provided by title companies are:

- Property profile information
- eFarm/database of properties and owners' names in a target area
- Real estate settlement and closing services (escrow) and tax deferred exchanges
- Due diligence assistance on title-related issues
- Property exchanges and intermediary services
- Preliminary and final title reports, sometimes called an abstract of title

Investors need reliable advice and help throughout the acquisition of new properties for their commercial real estate investment portfolio, though most commercial real estate investors will not need help in each specific resource area identified. It should also be noted that each state has unique legal requirements that can impact the services that are provided by title companies. Some of the most involved and important title company resources are described below in more detail.

Property Profile

The title company can provide a unique report called a Property Profile which contains:

- Owner of record on title
- Where the property tax bill is sent
- The legal address
- The physical address
- The local Building and Safety Department data on the size of building, size of land, number of bedrooms and bathrooms, whether there is a pool, number of stories, zoning, current use, etc.
- Property transfer history and loans for current and previous owners, notices of default, inter-family transfers or dissolution transfers
- All the actual nearby (usually within a mile) sales comps recorded by the local county recorder's office for the last year for properties of this type and size
- Local property owners in the same area with the same category of property
- Plat map (if available)

eFarm (Database of Properties)

An eFarm is a database of specific properties based on a set of criteria including, but not limited to, owner's property location, property type, year built, square footage of building, and land size—either square footage or acreage. It's a great tool for searching for potential properties.

Real Estate Settlement and Closing Services (Escrow)

Title companies offer escrow services for settling and closing a transaction as an independent third party. Escrow services receive the signed purchase and sale agreement, signed by both the seller and the buyer, and then they turn the purchase and sale agreement into Escrow Instructions for both parties to sign. The Escrow Instructions spell out the duties and responsibilities of both the buyer and the seller. Escrow receives and holds, in trust, all deposits, including Ernest Money and other deposits, and wire transfers from the buyer's financial institution to finance the purchase. Escrow also gathers all necessary documentations, including but not limited to:

- Preliminary title report
- Title Company's final title report or abstract of title
- Insurance policies
- Leases (and perhaps abstracts of the leases) for the subject property
- All agreements and contracts for services, utility bills, and property tax bill

Escrow gathers all the transaction information, all monies, and loan proceeds for the transaction, then creates a closing statement that allocates and prorates the respective professional services, costs, bills, and taxes between the seller and the buyer as of the date of closing.

Upon the execution of the closing documents, deeds, mortgages, and/or trust deeds, they arrange to record the appropriate documents at the county recorder's office or another central depository. The last thing they do is to convey the proceeds of the sale to the seller and the deed and keys of the property to the buyer.

Note: Escrow services are particularly used in the Western United States instead of using a closing attorney, which is a common practice in the Eastern United States and across Canada.

Due Diligence Data Gathering

It is common for commercial real estate purchase contracts to include many of the due diligence items requested by the buyer. The title company escrow process is the normal place for exchanging this material that is critical to fulfilling requirements requested and agreed to in the purchase contract.

Property Exchanges and Intermediary Services

Investors will only use this specialized title company resource if they are involved in a tax-deferred exchange. While most commercial property transfers involve a buyer and a seller for one business property such as an apartment or office building, there are some specialized variations such as tax-deferred exchanges that involve the exchange of one property for another in a specific legal process that enables a unique tax treatment that is beneficial to both parties. The presence of multiple commercial properties makes this a more complicated transaction, and this is an excellent illustration of a helpful resource provided by some (but not all) title companies' escrow offices.

A tax-deferred exchange requires the presence of a qualified intermediary, but there can also be other specialized real estate transactions that will be facilitated by the presence of a third party (intermediary) acting in a neutral capacity. Due diligence requirements and many other actions that are performed during escrow will usually proceed more smoothly with the direct involvement of an intermediary. Title companies' escrow offices are ideally suited to fulfill this important role and can be most helpful with title-related due diligence issues.

These real estate exchanges are usually referred to as "1031 tax deferred exchanges" because they are regulated by the provisions of Section 1031 in the U.S. Internal Revenue Code. Title companies, which are well-prepared to assist with these transactions, usually have established divisions that act as a "1031 exchange qualified intermediary."

Note: Per the IRS 1031 regulations, if you are going to do a 1031 exchange you must use an intermediary that you have not recently done business with.

Preliminary and Final Title Reports

As suggested by its name, a title report (both preliminary and final versions) is an investor resource area that is particularly appropriate to be handled by a title company. A commercial property owner always wants a "clear title" and title companies are uniquely qualified to provide this service.

A preliminary title report is customarily provided as a preview of conditions, terms, and exceptions that will eventually be included in a title insurance policy. It is not unusual for some of the exceptions to be unexpected, and the preliminary nature of this title report enables all parties to question and investigate further whenever appropriate.

A Professional Network

There's much more to title companies than the title search, of course. Another possibility you might consider when talking to your title company of choice is asking it to provide you with referrals within its own network of customers and partners. The fact is, other commercial real estate professionals within your local community are likely using the title company each day, so you might be able to find good prospects for commercial brokers, lenders, and other investors to consult with through the title company. The title company might also have ties to member organizations worth considering.

Ultimately, finding and analyzing commercial property is a complex and multi-faceted process. You won't necessarily want to rely on any one source for the information you need to get the job done, but instead, gather the most useful information from various sources to give you a broader perspective of the local commercial real estate economy and how best to proceed. From the main functions of a title company to its unique vantage point in the commercial real estate market, you can find plenty of highly-beneficial assistance from your chosen title company. Take the information and referrals you get from there as a good launching point for your next real estate deal.

I have used Chicago Title Company for forty years. And for the last twenty-five years have had the good fortune to have the same amazing title representative; she is an invaluable member of my commercial real estate team.

Chapter 19

How to Find and Hire a Good Commercial Property Manager

Effective property management is one of the most important factors in any successful commercial real estate investment. In most cases, property management is equal in importance to the initial due diligence and acquisition phase. What makes the property management requirement especially critical and unique in importance is its long-term role in enhancing income, equity build-up, and long-term capital appreciation for apartments and other commercial properties.

The search and hiring process for a commercial property manager or commercial property management company should run in parallel with the investment acquisition phase. You need to produce a satisfactory candidate. Prudent investors should be prepared to pursue alternative and traditional strategies for assembling an effective property management team. Additionally, there can be circumstances in which property managers must be replaced after the purchase has been completed. Regardless of whether it will be necessary to hire and find a property manager at the inception of ownership or several years later, this practical personnel requirement cannot be and should not be overlooked.

As with any commercial real estate expert's help, property management services are not free. The cost can vary significantly depending on the scope of work needed. The costs will usually be expressed as a percentage of monthly gross income for a property, but other financial arrangements, such as a fixed salary, are also possible. A working range will start at around 8 to10 percent of collected rents plus a commission or fee for leasing a unit. They may take one month's rent (upfront) on a new apartment lease and usually charge a fee or surcharge on any repairs they order and/or oversee. Find out upfront how much these fees vary.

To assess the possibilities of hiring a property manager, it will be helpful to identify what an investor wants and needs to be accomplished by this key person or company. Here is an abbreviated summary of several normal responsibilities that belong on this list:

- Maintenance and repair
- Finding new tenants as vacancies occur
- Handling tenant complaints
- Evicting tenants as needed
- Collecting rent
- Managing a building budget and paying all operating expenses
- Recording and submitting financial information
- Qualifying possible tenants
- Negotiating new leases
- Handling lease renewals
- Overseeing property repairs
- Screening and hiring contractor to do repairs
- Disbursing to the owner the net income

Existing Property Management Might Not Need to Be Changed

When investors buy multifamily housing properties or any other commercial real estate, there might already be a viable property manager, or property management company, in place. The due diligence process will provide valuable insights about the effectiveness of the current property management team and ideally should also identify whether they are available for hire by new owners.

On the other hand, poor property management could also lead to a buying opportunity that involves changing commercial property managers, or the property management company, at the earliest possible opportunity after purchase in order to turn around an investment that has been mismanaged.

Review Property Managers While Considering Whether to Invest

During the due diligence phase, some properties might be eliminated, or continued, from further consideration even though they have been well managed. It is wise to remember the strong points of these property managers when and if an investor needs property management help. Seeing them in action by evaluating their financial and managerial capabilities can be the best possible form of an early job interview.

Get Referrals from Real Estate Experts

While dealing with real estate professionals, such as commercial real estate brokers, real estate attorneys, architects, title companies, and construction companies, a forward-looking investor will take plenty of notes about various experts that have either been recommended or mentioned in a negative manner. As mentioned above, if you do not currently need a new property manager, or property management firm, you may in the future.

Search the Internet

In a business world that has an ongoing partnership with technology and real-time data, the internet search engines will always have a seat at the table when real estate professionals are looking for more information about people and properties. Even after an investor has located what appears to be the "perfect" property manager (which might be the current property manager), it is natural and appropriate to perform due diligence regarding such a key individual or company. The internet is one source to find information about current and prospective property management personnel.

Bring Your Own Property Management Team

Some investors will already know (or think they know) who they want to do this. It might be someone already performing similar duties at your existing investment properties. Even if this is the case, it is still advisable to consider all other available choices for managing your newest acquisition.

Professional Property Management Organizations

In many professional fields, there are organizations that provide advanced training and credentials to establish levels of expertise. One that is relevant to the current discussion is the Institute of Real Estate Management (IREM). This is the only such organization that currently serves both commercial and multifamily sectors. Various credentials are offered by IREM, including Certified Property Manager (CPM) and Accredited Residential Manager (ARM).

Summary: Who Are the Best Potential Property Managers for Commercial Real Estate?

- Existing property managers
- Property managers at other purchase property candidates
- A manager that you bring
- You
- Referrals from real estate professionals
- One found via an internet search
- One found through property management organizations
- IREM members (CPM and ARM designations)

IREM members (CPM and ARM designations)

As with any other investment and management decision, property management plans and results should be reviewed periodically. As circumstances change, property manager requirements might also need to be revised.

How to Select a Commercial Real Estate Manager or Management Firm

When you select a property manager, you want to first look for contacts in your area—or more importantly, the area where your investment properties are located. You can make inquiries for recommended managers from any realtors or title companies you know.

Prior to hiring a commercial property manager, find out how many properties they are, or have managed previously. Ask them to calculate the total number of units they manage as well as the vacancy rate of those units. Their vacancy rate should be close to, or less than, the current regional rates.

If your regional rate is under two percent and the potential property manager has a vacancy rate of ten percent or more, this should be a huge red flag.

The Investigation

Verify how prompt the potential manager is with communication with existing tenants or lessees. Call them as a potential renter for a space they have listed. See how quickly they respond to any message you send, how knowledgeable they are, and how promptly they can show a property. This experience will give you a good idea as to their service level and knowledge level.

While verifying their work, drive by some of the properties they manage and see how well the space is maintained. Verify whether they have had multiple complaints filed against them via the Better Business Bureau (BBB). Don’t be put off by a handful of complaints—there are always a few angry people for every good business out there. However, a good property manager will respond to those complaints. But, if there is an abnormal amount, it is a big red flag.

The Interview

Once you have narrowed down your list of prospective property managers and/or property management firms, you will need to interview them. Each one will have their own practiced sales pitch, but it is important to ask a few questions including:

- How many units do you manage?
- What is your specialty? (i.e. commercial, multifamily)

- How long have you been in business?
- Are you in good standing with the BBB?
- How many employees do you have?
- Do you have a current valid real estate license? (Most states require property managers to have real estate licenses)
- What are your standard rates for property management?
- Are there extra leasing fees for a new tenant, if so, how much?
- Do you have monetary affiliations with your contractors? (Some states require that property managers disclose any kickbacks received by contractors)
- Do you personally own properties? What kind? (If their company manages fifty properties and they personally own thirty-five of them, they are likely going to rent theirs first)
- What type of insurance do you have? (Good property managers should have errors and omission insurance, as well as general liability insurance)
- What charges are added to construction repairs or maintenance invoices?
- What is your fee or surcharge on repairs or contractor's charges?
- Are you and/or your firm a member of IREM?
- Do you have anyone with a CPM or ARM designations?

IREM Is a Great Source for Property Managers

The professional association for property managers and property management firms is IREM (www.IREM.org). IREM is a branch of the National Association of Realtors (NAR), which awards the Certified Property Manager (CPM) designation to experience, trained, and qualified property managers.

Do It Yourself

If the "do it yourself" option is under serious consideration, it is important to review what it means to be an investor rather than a commercial property manager. Do you want to do both? Before going down this path, it should be preceded by doing your own due diligence about what is required and what could go wrong along the way. Be smart—hire a professional property manager or firm.

Chapter 20

What Is a CCIM?

Acronyms can be a challenge when individuals are getting involved with any new field or interest. It might seem that specialized topics have more than their fair share of unique terms and acronyms. It is true that commercial real estate has an abundance of special terminology, and successful commercial real estate investors should take the time to become familiar and comfortable with the most critical words and concepts in the world of commercial property investments, such as apartments and office buildings.

To accomplish this mission efficiently and effectively, a smart investor should consider which one or two (or more) commercial real estate investment experts are most likely to help them achieve their investing goals. One prudent answer to this challenge is contained within one of the most prominent acronyms that will always be important when discussing commercial real estate: CCIM.

A Brief History of CCIM

For those who like to hear the words behind the acronym, CCIM refers to Certified Commercial Investment Member. The CCIM Institute was founded in 1954 and has six decades of rich history in advancing commercial real estate to its current respected position of international prominence.

The CCIM Institute is currently based in Chicago. The full (and official) name of this global leader in commercial real estate education and services is The CCIM Institute of the National Association of REALTORS®. The CCIM Institute is legally established as a 501(c)(6) trade association. Their website (http://www.ccim.com) is appropriately consistent with the acronym.

What Does CCIM Mean to Commercial Real Estate Investors?

A commercial real estate professional who bears the designation as a CCIM must undergo a lengthy and involved certification process. Through a combination of proven skills and experiences, someone who has earned the CCIM title is a certified expert in their chosen field. This official acknowledgment of commercial real estate expertise should be invaluable to any investor seeking to succeed in their investment strategies.

No matter whether someone is investing in real estate or some other business opportunity, there is always an ongoing challenge to find "experts" who can help investors achieve financial success. There is rarely a shortage of individuals who regularly refer to themselves as a "commercial real estate expert." It is only natural to question such claims of expertise in the absence of any tangible proof.

The CCIM designation is one of the best possible objective indicators that an investor has located a valid and certified commercial property investment expert. On that score alone, CCIM becomes an acronym worth remembering for any forward-thinking real estate investor.

Ethics is another area that is often difficult for any investor to measure when they are evaluating which commercial real estate professionals to include on their investment team. The CCIM Institute has included adherence to demanding ethical standards and practices as among the most important part of the CCIM certification procedures.

How Can a Commercial Property Investor Benefit Directly by Working with a CCIM?

There are several unique services available exclusively to Certified Commercial Investment Members, and these services in turn allow a CCIM to provide valuable information to their investor clients. Here are a few examples, some of which do involve additional acronyms (each will be explained in additional detail below):

- CCIM Institute MailBridge
- CCIMREDEX
- STDBonline
- CCIMQTM

The CCIM Institute MailBridge information-sharing service allows members to share property haves and wants with the CCIM member network. In a real-world environment where networking is often the practical pathway for accomplishing difficult tasks more effectively and consistently, this dedicated communication tool for sharing commercial real estate investment information can have exceptional value for investors.

CCIMREDEX is a service designed to serve as a real estate data exchange. Investment success often depends on who has the right data at the right time, and the CCIM Institute has recognized the unique importance of this valuable commodity by providing its designated members with special access to such information.

STDBonline is a site that helps CCIMs do business online. The ability to achieve commercial real estate investment success increasingly depends on site-specific demographics and reports that are made available on an exclusive basis through this online data site to members of the CCIM Institute.

CCIMQTM provides CCIM real estate experts with quarterly market trends for the top forty-eight markets in the United States. As with any investment, it is critical to consistently monitor and analyze changes in financial data over time. These quarterly reports for major concentrations of U.S. commercial real estate will usually prove to be invaluable for any successful commercial real estate investor.

Final Words about Certified Commercial Investment Members

The CCIM Institute has gone to great lengths to make the CCIM designation a particularly meaningful one for both those who have earned (or aspire to earn) the CCIM designation and investors who are constantly searching for effective and ethical experts to help them in their ongoing quest for commercial real estate investment excellence. The CCIM Institute is always perfecting their standards in the following areas:

- Education
- News
- Theory and Application
- Networking

- Ethics
- Information

Serving Clients

A CCIM has extensive education and proven experience in commercial real estate that has proven to be a powerful combination. To earn their coveted "CCIM" designation CCIMs have:

- Many years of experience in commercial real estate
- Listed, sold, or purchased in commercial real estate:

  Three (3) or more qualifying activities totaling $30 million or more, OR; 2. Exactly ten (10) qualifying activities that must total $10 million or more, OR; 3. Twenty (20) qualifying activities without regard to total dollar volume
- Taken a series of extensive and intensive courses on every aspect of commercial real estate
- Documented their closed commercial real estate transaction
- Successfully taken a comprehensive exam on all aspects of commercial real estate.

Chapter 21

Value of a Commercial Real Estate Mentor

Accelerate and Enhance Your Success

A commercial real estate mentor can help a prospective or experienced commercial investor accelerate and improve their success and give them "real world," in-the-field experience as a "cap-stone" event in their commercial real estate investing education.

A book (such as this one), a specialized commercial real estate course, a series of webinars, or CDs are available to lay out the groundwork and provide important foundational commercial real estate knowledge and commercial real estate investing background.

However, a personal one-on-one commercial real estate mentor, in addition to the basic and advanced commercial real estate training, can and should be engaged for a one-on-one mentorship in the field to truly complete an investor's education and launch their career as a commercial real estate investor.

An effective commercial real estate mentor will share their expertise and knowledge, and help with deal selection, analysis, offer to help prep and negotiate your deal either on the phone or in person (in the field).

Extensive "Real World" Experience

If you are considering becoming a professional commercial real estate investor, you'll need a mentor with extensive "real world" experience. You will need someone who has been a successful commercial real estate investor themselves, someone who understands every aspect of commercial real estate investing:

- Identification of potential properties
- Analysis
- Due Diligence
- Contracts
- Offers
- Negotiation
- Finance
- Closings
- Ownership

A professional commercial real estate mentor will have practical and proven experience in all the various types of commercial real estate investing, including but not limited to:

- Apartments
- Offices
- Industrial
- Retail malls
- Warehouses
- Self-storage units
- Strip retail

- Shopping centers
- Medical buildings
- Mobile home parks
- Trucking terminals
- Mixed use (Commercial)
- Residential over retail
- Industrial with or without office space
- Specialty commercial real estate

Dedicated to Your Success

A professional commercial real estate mentor should be dedicated to your success. He or she should have a solid knowledge of and can mentor/coach a mentee on how to find, qualify for, and build a commercial real estate team. Commercial real estate teams include the following:

- Commercial real estate brokers
- Commercial real estate websites
- Commercial real estate mortgage brokers
- Commercial real estate appraisers
- Commercial real estate property managers
- Title reps who understand commercial real estate and who can provide information to the commercial real estate mentee
- Tax professionals (CPA, or Chartered Accountant) who know and specialize in commercial real estate and who can do more than a tax return or financial statement
- "Street-Smart" commercial real estate attorneys (for advice on contracts and other legal matters)

- Title companies and title representatives
- Escrow companies or closing attorneys (depending on the locations and needs)
- General contractors and specialty sub-contractors (including how to find, screen, and engage them)
- Commercial property inspectors who are totally independent from the commercial real estate agents (I personally like a "street-smart junkyard dog" commercial inspector who will find out everything and know how to create a report for the prospective buyer with all the facts)
- CCIMs (as necessary)

A commercial real estate mentor needs to be engaged and dedicated to his or her mentee during phone coaching sessions and/or in the field during their one-on-one meetings. A commercial real estate mentor needs to be able to teach, guide, mentor, motivate, inspire, "lead by example," and provide key "real world" commercial real estate insights. A mentor should also be able to provide written notes on key points, as well as give sample dialogs between the mentee and sellers, brokers, lenders, mortgage brokers, and other team members.

A commercial real estate mentor needs to have excellent communication skills and patience with a deep desire to mentor, guide, teach, and inspire mentees toward success.

The prospective commercial real estate mentee should check out what the mentor's previous mentees shared in writing or in videos, testimonials, or recommendations about experiences with the commercial real estate mentor.

Chapter 22

What Is Required for Commercial Real Estate Due Diligence?

Due diligence is arguably one of the most important phases for any investor who wants to either begin or expand their commercial real estate portfolio. The primary purpose of due diligence is to gather all the available data and then to review, reconcile, audit, investigate, and verify as much information as possible prior to closing the purchase.

The most successful commercial real estate investors understand the vital role of due diligence and consistently use it as a tool for managing risk and preventing unnecessary harm to their legal and financial interests. If that sounds like the bar is set at a high level for what investors should expect from due diligence, that is indeed the case. Due diligence is that important and critical for commercial real estate investors.

When Does Due Diligence Begin for Commercial Real Estate Purchases?

In many cases the due diligence process will begin before an offer to purchase an investment or commercial property has been made, and in such situations, the preliminary steps will be instrumental in identifying primary purchase candidates. It is rarely possible to obtain all financial and legal information in the earliest stages of the commercial real estate investment process.

The most intensive portions of due diligence are typically reserved for the period that begins with an offer to purchase apartments or other commercial properties. The LOI (Letter of Intent), or formal offer to purchase, should be as specific as possible in terms of all the financials and documentation that will be required to complete all due diligence requirements prior to closing.

Prior to entering a legal agreement for sale of a commercial property, many sellers are understandably reluctant to provide personal and confidential information to prospective buyers. In circumstances where an earlier receipt of data is requested by an investor (prior to submitting a purchase offer), you may need to sign a variation of a confidentiality or "nondisclosure agreement" (NDA). But even with a legally-enforceable NDA, serious due diligence audits and verifications might need to be postponed until an offer to purchase from the buyer/investor has been formally accepted by a seller.

Title Company Commercial Property Profile

One of the earliest sources of investigation (even before the offer) is likely to involve what is generally referred to as a title company "property profile." This data is available from online databases and provides a wealth of preliminary data about a property such as deed, zoning, comparable sales, and title information.

Title Company Commercial Property Preliminary Title Report

It is always helpful to know as much as possible in advance about a property of interest, and property profiles are one of the most useful tools for early investment decisions. The information gathered before the formal "purchase offer and acceptance" can be referred to as "preliminary due diligence." Whatever this stage is called, it will usually include a title company property profile for various investment properties under consideration by an investor.

This preliminary phase will also typically include informal discussions with sellers regarding the availability of documents and information that a prospective buyer may request as part of a formal purchase offer. You can also order a Preliminary Title Report up front that can be helpful even though it contains only the "raw data" and is not a Final Title Report.

Due Diligence Requirements in a Purchase Contract

An important part of any due diligence process is to identify which records and documents need to be examined. It is then critical to include those requirements in any legally-binding purchase contract. Commercial real estate investors will typically rely on the advice and counsel from their attorney and commercial real estate experts when preparing an offer to purchase their next investment property. Here is a list of documents to consider for inclusion in this phase of due diligence:

- Current title policy (previous)
- All leases for current tenants and lease summaries
- Utility bills
- All operation agreements and contracts
- Insurance policies
- All financial records (tax returns and financial statements for the last three years)
- Commercial property inspections

- Permits and zoning
- Local tax records
- Environmental research (EIR I, II, or III)
- Interviews with neighbors and tenants
- All legal contracts in effect for the property
- New preliminary and final title report
- Estoppel; Certificates from all existing tenants
- Anything else that is considered material to the sale

There is usually a "entire full due diligence period" defined in a formal purchase agreement. Gathering more information about a commercial property such as an apartment or office building could conceivably go on indefinitely if the buyer and seller did not mutually agree to a reasonable period to gather and assess all relevant data. Many of the items to be audited and verified require the complete cooperation of the selling party. It is not unusual for involved parties to extend the period included in the original purchase contract because required documentation was not provided in a timely manner. What is involved in the due diligence process is not defined, so the buyer may include all issues, items, or documents reviews.

When intermediary services such as real property exchanges are involved, the due diligence process becomes even more complex. With a commercial real estate exchange, the required inspections and verification of records now involves multiple properties and locations. Possible legal and administrative complications can be minimized by the inclusion of experienced and trusted commercial real estate experts and an experienced, knowledgeable intermediary/exchange company.

The Role of Escrow and Title Companies in Due Diligence

As always, due diligence will proceed more smoothly when facilitated by a title company and title company escrow that knows about common escrow problems of all kinds that can be avoided with prudent planning in advance. In any case, escrow is a specific process that is typically mandated by legal statutes in effect for most real estate transfers. The laws and regulations governing escrow can vary from one state to another. Even when escrow is not legally required, all prudent investors should welcome the opportunity to have much of the complicated due diligence process facilitated by a title insurance company that is managing escrow. Most of the eastern U.S. and Canada use closing attorneys (rather than escrows.)

Some Final Words about Commercial Real Estate Due Diligence

Despite the strong role played by title insurance companies, investors, and their complete investment teams ultimately bear full responsibility for completing the entire full due diligence requirements to the complete satisfaction of the buyers. High expectations by commercial real estate investors are always appropriate whenever any aspect of the due diligence process is involved. Possible shortcuts and expedited closing procedures should not be approved by buyers of apartments and other commercial properties unless they are comfortable that the due diligence checklist has been properly fulfilled per their expectations.

What Is Required to Gather All the Information and Conduct Due Diligence?

After being involved in commercial real estate investing, even tangentially, you've probably heard the term "due diligence" thrown around quite a bit. This term sounds complicated, but it simply refers to the process of evaluating a commercial property you've got under contract. To do this properly, you need to find out a lot of information and confirm that everything is in the condition you expected when you decided to purchase the property. While the length of a proper due diligence checklist is often intimidating, it's crucial you go over each item to make sure you aren't buying yourself a huge problem instead of a profitable property.

The Physical Inspection

It's important to remember that it's the buyer's responsibility to evaluate a commercial property, because the types of laws that protect residential homebuyers rarely apply in commercial property transactions. The first step on your due diligence agenda, then, is to conduct a physical inspection of the property you're buying. You're going to be looking at the physical condition of the property itself.

Whether it's an office building, a retail shopping center, or apartments, you'll need to inspect the foundation, walls, roof, windows, plumbing, parking lots, air conditioning, electrical, and any other applicable systems. If you aren't qualified to inspect everything on your own, find professionals who are. The money you spend on inspections will be worth it if they find anything bad enough to be a deal-breaker, and it's also worth paying them to give you a realistic assessment of the property's physical condition for future reference.

The Financial Investigation

The physical inspection is probably the costliest and most important due diligence aspect, but financial investigation is also highly important. To begin with, you can't take anything the seller says at face value. You'll need to approach the seller directly and ask for all their relevant financial records, including three years of income and expense statements and the property's current balance sheet. These will tell you about the annual income and expenses of the property, as well as the overall assets and liabilities associated with it. You need to get to the actual Net Operating Income (the NOI) for the last three years.

Other critical financial information includes property taxes, which you can double-check with the county assessor, and utility bills, which you can double-check with each respective utility company. Also, look at tax returns, rent rolls, lease agreements, and lease summaries. You should be able to get all this information from the seller, and it's worth taking a step back and reconsidering the entire deal if the necessary financial documentation is unavailable. Some sellers are guarded about releasing tax returns, but, as a prudent investor, you should insist on receiving them. You don't need the entire Federal tax return, such as their personal 1040, only the schedule E or their LLC's tax returns for the subject property.

The Legal Inquiries

As complicated as the physical inspection and financial investigation can be, considering the legal aspect of commercial property is perhaps the most complex. It begins with the environmental inspection and reports (EIR), an assessment of the past use of the property that references any environmental liabilities. You need a survey and title inspection, which verify that the property dimensions are accurate, as well as reveal any liens or judgments still in effect. If there are any issues, you'll have to insist the seller clear them ***before*** proceeding to close.

As part of the legal inquiry, it's up to you to check on zoning for the property to make sure it's not in violation. Seek out the insurance claims history to see what sorts of claims were taken out for things like fire and floods, as well as any lapses in coverage. While you're at it, it's often a good idea to get in touch with your local police department and find out if the property has any past or current problems with the law enforcement. The thing is, these are issues the seller might not necessarily be upfront in disclosing, but you want to know about before you take on full ownership of the property and its problems.

The Seller's Reputation

If you're about ready to pull the trigger and proceed to close the deal, you might consider one more aspect of due diligence. In a local community, a seller's reputation could mean the difference between a successful commercial real estate career and a poor one. That's why it's sometimes appropriate to do a bit of due diligence on the person or company from whom you're purchasing a commercial property. Even if the property seems to be in good standing, with everything checking out, sometimes a perusal into the seller can reveal some inconsistencies or issues that help you avoid a mistake. Information about the seller is usually accessible through public government records.

Once you've gone through this lengthy process of due diligence, you should have an accurate picture of the property's pros and cons. Only then should you move forward with the deal, because you'll have all the knowledge to make an informed, intelligent business decision that owning the commercial property can still be profitable!

Chapter 23

Conducting a Strategic Commercial Real Estate Investment Analysis

No matter what type of commercial real estate you plan to invest in—whether it's industrial, apartments, office, or retail—there are several key areas you need to analyze thoroughly before pulling the trigger on the purchase. You can do this but don't make it a doctoral dissertation. Just gather the necessary information to get a good feel about the property.

There are seven important areas to investigate:

1. Specific market and competitive analyses

The first thing you need to evaluate for any commercial property you are considering is the market in the location of the property. Is there a demand in the area for the property you're buying? If you're considering purchasing an apartment, you need to look at the occupancy rates of other properties in the area. Are they at or near capacity? What are the current lease rates? Will you be able to keep your occupancy rates at or near capacity, and will you be able to charge a rent rate high enough to earn the return you need to make the property profitable?

2. Political, demographic, and legal analyses

What is the political, demographic, and legal atmosphere in the area where you are considering acquiring a property? Are there any political policies that could affect the success of your investment? For instance, if you're considering an industrial property, has the local government dealt fairly and favorably toward commercial real estate? Has the local government been reluctant to work with real estate investors and developers or imposed legal hurdles that could make it more difficult to develop, purchase, and manage your property?

What about the demographics of the target region? If you're considering buying a senior citizen high rise, does the area have a growing population of retirement-age residents who will continue to drive up the demand—and the lease rates? It's important to take a close look at how the property you're considering will perform in the current and future environment—and whether the local political officials will be willing to work with you to help your property succeed, or will they be more likely to throw up impediments to your success.

3. Property location and site analyses

What kind of location is the commercial property located in? If you're interested in a property in an office or industrial park, you need to know if it is thriving and near capacity or if it is run-down with declining occupancy? If it's an apartment complex, is it in a good neighborhood with favorable rent rates, or is it in a depressed part of town with declining or stagnant rates? How are the occupancy rates in the area?

Nearly any property can be a suitable investment at the right price, but it's important to get a complete picture of the property location to determine suitable value.

A thorough site analysis is important. What is the condition of the property? Is it ready to go or will it require substantial investment to attract new tenants? Explore the environmental condition of the area as well as any zoning issues you could potentially face.

Utilities are also important. How is access to the water supply as well as to electricity and other utilities? Make sure everything is in order before you consider buying the property.

4. Detailed property financial analysis

How has the property done financially over the past three years? The seller or broker will likely provide you with a pro forma that should include key financials such as cash flow, a balance sheet, investor performance, return on investment, and income and expenses. Ask for the actual historical financials for the last three years. Do not accept pro formas or work papers; get the real financial details. Get a minimum of three years of actual income and expenses for the property. Nothing else is acceptable. Be firm. Do not accept pro formas or excuses.

Don't take their word for it. You should meet with your accountant to examine the last three years of books (actual numbers), if possible, to see if the pro forma or summary of numbers coincide with reality. If it sounds too good to be true, you must wonder why the current owner is trying to sell it. Look at everything with a skeptical eye.

Look at all of the actual historic expenses and recent improvement costs as well as occupancy rates and revenue generated by rental income over the past three years. Also, study the trends. Research as to whether the occupancy rate improved or declined over the three-year period, and check out total revenues. Are they going up, going down, or have they remained about the same throughout the past three years? That will give you a good indication of how the property will perform after you buy it. It's important to know everything possible about the last three years' actual financial performance of a property before you invest.

5. Economics (local, national, and even global)

Economics can have a significant effect on commercial and residential income property prices. A booming economy will drive prices up, while a declining economy will drive prices down. The local economy is probably the most important indicator, but the national and world economies can also influence property prices. You don't want to overpay for a commercial property in a declining economy.

Commercial and industrial properties can be affected significantly by an economic slump. On the other hand, the recent housing crisis turned out to be a boon for rental properties, as single-family property ownership declined and more people opted to rent rather than buy homes.

6. Technology and lifestyle

If you're considering buying an apartment, you should ask if it has ready access to internet, cable TV, and other technologies important to today's consumers. Is it located in an area that is convenient to shopping, restaurants, bus lines, and other services? Consumers love their technology and they love conveniences. Renters also like amenities within their own complex, such as a swimming pool, work-out facility, party or meeting rooms, and laundry areas. Your property will perform better if it provides the means for a vibrant lifestyle.

For industrial properties, technology and access to transportation, such as rail lines and highways, is essential. Office and retail properties also require access to proper technology and easy access for consumers as well as ADA (handicapped)compliancy regulations.

7. Current demand versus current inventory

No matter what condition the property is in, where it's located, or how profitable it has been over the past few years, future demand is still an essential key to the future success of the property. You need to gauge the current demand versus the current inventory. You also need to take a close look at new and pending property developments in the area. Are there new industrial or office parks or apartments planned or currently under construction in the area that could affect occupancy rates for the property you are considering to buy? Are there new shopping centers going up that could drive business from the retail property you're considering? Or is there a growing demand for the type of space you're considering? These are all factors that could affect the value of the property and its future revenue.

Assessing the value of a property can be a very tedious and time-consuming process, but these factors are important in determining the value of the property and the price you should be willing to pay for it. If it all adds up, you may have a great property for investment. If not, your best option may be to move on to the next prospective property. My four-letter word for that is "NEXT!"

Chapter 24

Celebrating the Many Differences and Benefits of Commercial Loans

Despite the ups and downs in investment markets during the past fifty years, one constant has remained: A commercial loan continues to be the primary financial tool for buying commercial property of all kinds—ranging from apartments to office buildings, retail shopping centers, golf courses, self-storage units, industrial buildings, restaurants, and mobile home parks.

It is, of course, true that the rules and regulations surrounding commercial lending have been modified over the years. Nevertheless, many things remain the same—here are a few examples:

- Commercial buyers have many alternative sources to consider when obtaining a business loan to buy commercial property—banks are only one stop on the commercial loan shopping list. Hire a good commercial mortgage broker to help you obtain the best financing.
- Income (especially the NOI) is of paramount importance when buying commercial real estate—in addition to "location, location, and location," commercial real estate investors should add "NOI, NOI, and NOI."
- Commercial lenders look critically at the Net Operating Income (NOI).

- Commercial lenders use "debt service coverage ratio" (DSCR) or similar variations to analyze debt and income for a commercial property—this underwriting standard is a helpful reminder to commercial borrowers about the delicate balance between net operating income and debt service.
- The different kinds of commercial property involve different lending standards—properties such as apartments typically involve less investment risk, lower interest rates, longer terms, and higher loan-to-value.
- Commercial loans usually involve buildings occupied by businesses rather than individual families—major exceptions include apartments and mobile home parks, and lenders are often more willing to lend on residential properties.

Multiple Sources for Commercial Loans

With commercial lending, traditional banks are not the "only game in town." While commercial borrowers should always see if banking institutions are competitive, don't overlook some non-traditional sources as well—life insurance companies, pension funds, mezzanine lenders, conduit lenders, capital companies, savings and loans, credit unions, and hard money lenders are common examples.

While borrowers should complete their due diligence concerning the property, an equally important item on the due diligence list is to examine potential lenders carefully before signing any commercial loan agreements. It is prudent to always have a "Plan B" (and "Plan C") lender in mind if the original source of financing falls through unexpectedly. One or more lenders saying "No" before one says "Yes" is often normal and to be expected in today's commercial lending climate.

What Is the Debt Coverage Ratio?

The DSCR or debt service coverage ratio is how commercial lenders express the relationship between NOI and debt service. The DSCR is derived by dividing net operating income by total debt service. A DSCR of more than 1.2 is always important because it means that the net income exceeds the debt service payments.

Because lenders and borrowers should both be prepared for "something to go wrong" when managing a property, the DSCR needs to be 1.2 to 1.5 so that the net operating income is significantly higher than the debt service. This will ideally allow borrowers to deal with unexpected vacancies and property repairs without impacting the ability to make commercial loan payments on time.

Apartment Loans Are Often Easier to Obtain

Because commercial lending for apartments is significantly different from other commercial loans, buying apartment properties is frequently the "smart thing to do" for both novices and experienced investors. Not only are interest rates typically much lower for buying an apartment property, but higher leverage is also usually possible, a higher loan-to-value (LTV) in large part because both apartment loan borrowers and lenders have less perceived risk than with most other forms of commercial financing. Apartments also have lower DSCR of 1.2 to 1.3, which helps.

I remind you that it is in your best interest to get a good commercial mortgage broker. They can help secure the best financing for your commercial real estate deal.

A Final Comment: Expect to Need Some Expert Help

While some investors might prefer to do everything, this is rarely the most effective route for achieving maximum success with commercial real estate investing, and obtaining the best commercial loan. Commercial property investors will often need several experts. Key examples include a commercial real estate broker, a commercial real estate accountant, a commercial real estate attorney, a commercial property manager, and a commercial mortgage broker. A great online commercial real estate loan resource is scotsmanguide.com.

Remember that a commercial loan agreement is an intermediate or long-term legal document. Commercial property investors need proper legal advice from their commercial real estate attorney before signing anything. But first, investors should expect to need some help in finding a suitable commercial lender. Commercial real estate investing is a team effort!

Chapter 25

Advantages of Mezzanine Financing to Acquire Commercial Real Estate

Good news; banks and other lenders are beginning to loosen the purse strings, although many commercial real estate borrowers have had to become a little more creative in structuring debt deals.

Much of the capital for commercial real estate loans has come from two potent and powerful sources. Insurance companies and pension funds are looking for high, stable returns with minimal risk. With historically low yields from government bonds, both insurance companies and pension funds have become increasingly interested in funding commercial real estate deals to significantly bolster their income stream through a much higher return on investment.

Insurance companies and pension funds do not regularly loan directly to private investors and real estate investment groups; they typically participate in the market by providing capital directly to banks, mortgage brokers, mortgage bankers, and other lending organizations who, in turn, lend the pension fund and insurance company's money to the borrowers.

Many traditional loans are limited to 60 to 80 percent of the acquisition costs, leaving undercapitalized borrowers with the possible difficult task of securing additional funding to consummate their acquisitions.

Fortunately, there is another source of financing that can bridge that gap. "Mezzanine" financing has picked up dramatically in the past few years to help commercial real estate investors and developers make up the difference between their assets in hand and the loan amounts they can secure through traditional loans.

What Is Mezzanine Financing?

Mezzanine financing is used to raise additional capital to pay for real estate acquisitions that bridge the gap between the traditional mortgage and the investment group's capital in hand. While the traditional loan may cover in the range of 60 to 80 percent of the cost of the total commercial real estate investment, mezzanine financing can help the borrower finance up to 85 to 90 percent of the acquisition by providing the "gap" additional financing of 10 to 20 percent, which is subordinated to the traditional lenders' 60 to 80 percent loan.

But mezzanine financing is considered a subordinate obligation because the debt is repaid only after all other debt financing has been taken care of and remains in a secondary position, equivalent to a second Trust Deed or second mortgage, on their property lien behind the traditional first mortgage or first Trust Deed. The provider of the first mortgage (or first Trust Deed) has the first claim on cash flow, followed by mezzanine lenders, followed by equity investors, who receive the residual. If a borrower defaults, the mezzanine lender typically has the option of assuming the first mortgage obligation, or to simply walk away from the investment.

Because mezzanine loans are less secured and in a second position on both cash flow and lien position, mezzanine lenders charge a higher interest rate for these types of loans than the rates charged for more senior debt instruments. For instance, while a standard bank commercial real estate loan may carry an interest rate of six to eight percent, a mezzanine loan may cost the borrower 8 to 15 percent, or even more on riskier projects.

The pricing of loans typically increases as the leverage increases. Loans that approach 90 percent can significantly increase the cost for the borrower. That cost is often extracted in a possible equity position for the lender or pledges of additional collateral from the borrower.

The loan durations are also typically shorter with mezzanine loans, often in the range of only three to five years. However, some investment groups have been negotiating longer-term agreements for ten years to account for additional time required completing their exit objectives. This short-term mezzanine loan will usually result in a refinance of the commercial real estate in thirty to fifty months to pay off the mezzanine.

When structuring a mezzanine financing deal, you may want to negotiate an option for extending your loan duration beyond the initial three-to-five-year window. You may have to pledge additional collateral or equity in the project if you are forced to exercise the option, but having the option to extend the debt will give you more breathing room if the project doesn't proceed as quickly as the timeline you had projected it to.

The advantage of mezzanine debt, in addition to the obvious benefit of raising more money to reduce the equity requirement to purchase the property, is that it has the potential to increase equity returns and presents fewer limitations relative to the senior debt. By reducing the equity requirement, a borrower can lessen reliance on additional equity from additional partners. This gives borrowers the opportunity to maintain control of the investment and increase his or her share of the potential appreciation of the property, rather than sharing it with additional equity partners.

Structure a Deal

Mezzanine loans carry higher risks and higher loan rates than traditional mortgages. Mezzanine loan approval is routine if you can present a property with a favorable price that offers a high probability of delivering a suitable return on investment.

Like all financing, a mezzanine loan does not face losses unless the asset value of the property declines by an amount greater than the equity invested by the borrower.

Mezzanine loans are generally secured by the borrower's equity ownership in the property, rather than a secured lien on the property since that is typically held by the senior lender. Structuring the loan in this manner allows the lender to control the property more quickly in the case of foreclosure. The mezzanine lender may also negotiate an agreement with the senior lender that gives the mezzanine lender the right to address defaults, protect its investment, and assume the senior loan in the case of default.

Because of the risk of a mezzanine loan, lenders will require a very thorough analysis of the investment and a detailed assessment of the property value and potential income stream.

When you meet with a lender to discuss terms of the loan, come prepared. Be ready to document the property value and show cash flows from the property, as well as a well-conceived exit strategy.

Mezzanine lenders will assess the risk of your investment and adjust equity requirements accordingly, the greater the perceived risk, the greater the amount of equity required by the borrower, and often, the higher the interest rate.

To get a deal done with the most advantageous terms, you may be required to provide certain guarantees, letters of credit, cash flow sweeps, or assignment of rents, and deposits or reserves controlled by the lender. You may also decide to try to negotiate a longer-term deal than the typical three to five years for most mezzanine loans. However, negotiating a seven-to-ten-year term may possibly cost more in terms of interest rate hikes or additional collateral.

If you're not sure whether you'll need additional time to pay off the loan, a better choice might be to negotiate a loan for the shorter term with an option to extend the loan, if necessary, by including other incentives in the form of additional collateral or equity in the program.

Loans may be negotiated with either a fixed rate or floating rate that the lender may require you to protect against possible increases in market interest rates. You might be required to purchase interest rate caps or collars on both your senior and subordinated debt as part of a floating interest rate agreement.

With all the moving parts of a mezzanine loan, it would pay to negotiate with several potential lenders to see which one can provide the best combinations of terms.

Forms of Collateral

Mezzanine loans structured as debt instruments may require any one of several types of collateral. The most attractive to the lender would be a second deed of trust, or second mortgage, which allows the lender to foreclose on the property. If the owner defaults, in most cases, the senior lender would veto that type of arrangement.

Collateral can also be provided in the form of a partnership interest with the borrower. In that type of arrangement, the mezzanine lender would assume the borrower's equity in the property in the event of a default. As the new equity owner, the mezzanine lender would assume the obligations of the senior mortgage lender.

A third form of collateral is a cash flow note that gives the lender access to the cash flow from the property in the event of a default. However, it is subordinated to the first lien holder's assignment of rent clause.

When you're negotiating for a mezzanine loan, there are several key factors to consider. Come prepared with the proper documentation to provide a legitimate value of the property, the seller's asking price, the anticipated cash flow, and the projected income and the expenses to maintain the property. Be prepared to negotiate on several points, including duration of the loan (along with a possible option on an extension), the percentage of capital you will be required to cover, the amount of equity or other collateral you would have to put up, and the interest rate of the loan.

By negotiating with more than one lender, you can compare the specifics of each deal and determine the best option for your situation. Once you've determined the best offer based on all considerations, it's time to sign the loan agreement, close the deal, and begin the process of buying and managing your new property.

Chapter 26

How Cost Segregation Can Dramatically Increase Your Overall Return

Cost segregation is one of the most effective tools commercial real estate investors can use to maximize their depreciation and take advantage of tax benefits that can increase their net returns.

Cost segregation refers to the segregation of costs among structural components, personal property, and land improvements. With proper segregation, each component, including carpets, appliances, and other personal property, would be depreciated over the correct shorter tax life—which can provide several significant benefits for commercial real estate investors.

The two primary benefits to cost segregation include: 1) the ability to increase the property's cash flow by maximizing depreciation deductions in the early years and 2) the ability to defer income taxes to a later date. By deferring taxes, you'll receive more dollars today, providing you with a significant net present value benefit in the life cycle of the project. The ultimate result is that you would be able to lower the holding costs of your property, raise your cash flow, and maximize your investment returns.

Not everyone takes advantage of cost segregation, but there's no question that their bottom line could suffer. Very rarely would a property's entire cost be depreciated over the standard commercial real estate 39-year life, or 27.5-year life on apartments and other residential real estate, but some owners fail to take advantage of accelerated depreciation benefits of other components of their commercial property.

Although you typically pay a lump sum for the entire property when you make the initial purchase, there are many elements within the cost of the property that can be segregated for accelerated depreciation, including improvements made to the land and property and the personal property used by tenants that are not part of the structure of the building, such as stoves, refrigerators, carpeting, and other furnishings and fixtures.

By segregating the personal property and land improvements in their tax filings, property owners can achieve much faster depreciation for those items. Since a dollar in the hand today is worth a multiple of its future value thirty to forty years from now, it's in the investor's best interest to shield more of their money from taxes now, and pocket a higher portion of the returns.

The Federal Jobs and Growth Tax Relief Reconciliation Act allow property owners to take a first-year depreciation deduction equal to 50 percent of the basis of their qualified personal property. That can include tenant improvement allowances and certain allocations between the property owners and their tenants.

If you conduct your own cost segregation study, you should identify all the personal property in your rental building and determine its fair market value. For new property, you can use the actual value of each item at its price if purchased new. If the property is older, you would need to allow for wear and tear in determining a value. Whether you value your property through research on the internet or use an appraiser or cost segregation specialist, keep detailed records of your values and the means for your valuation in case you need to show them to the IRS at some future date. Once you've determined a fair value for your property, that becomes the tax basis for reporting and depreciating the property.

You may decide to cut back the time and effort you put into your cost segregation study by limiting it strictly to the big items, such as carpet, kitchen appliances, and washers and dryers, but the more property you can identify for accelerated depreciation, the greater the financial benefit you'll receive.

If you own a large property with many units, it may benefit you and help you avoid conflicts with the IRS, if you bring in a professional to perform your cost segregation study for you. There are financial experts and engineers who can conduct your cost segregation study to identify the appropriate items and assign them a fair market value. While that will add some extra costs to your operation, it could be well worth it based on the financial benefit you would reap. Usually the cost of retaining a professional cost segregation firm is recovered in the increased deductions they find and in knowing they have done everything correctly.

Whether you perform your own cost segregation analysis or hire an expert to do it for you, you will very likely find it to be well worth the effort. Otherwise, you'll be leaving a large pile of cash on the table.

Chapter 27

What Is an REIT?

Real estate investment trusts, known as REITs for short, are like stocks for the commercial real estate industry. They offer investors a simple, convenient way to buy a stake in the commercial real estate market around the world. There are more than 200 REITs that trade like stocks on the major stock exchanges.

Technically, REITs are trusts that buy commercial real estate properties, such as apartment buildings, office, and industrial properties, hotels, and shopping centers that produce income. When you buy shares in an REIT, you become a part owner in all the property holdings of the REIT.

Because they are traded like stocks, they provide the liquidity of stocks with the income potential of commercial real estate. They also often provide broad diversification because many REITs hold a variety of commercial properties.

First approved by Congress in 1960, REITs were slow to catch on initially, but they have become increasingly popular over the past two decades. You can buy any of the more than 200 REITs on the market through any broker and follow them in the daily stock listings.

For investors, REITs offer several attractive features. They typically pay among the highest yields of all types of investments, and the dividends often increase from year to year. And unlike real estate limited partnerships, they offer excellent liquidity since you can buy and sell them any time you wish, just like any stock on the major exchanges.

Types of REITs

There are several types of REITs. Many own and operate several types of commercial real estate, such as apartments, warehouses, office buildings, industrial sites, hotels, and shopping centers.

There are also specialized REITs that focus on a specific type of property. They may hold only apartments or shopping centers or only office buildings. There are also geographically-focused REITs that stick with a specific metropolitan area or geographic region. Others buy properties throughout the country.

There are also mortgage REITs that lend money to commercial real estate owners and operators, earning their profit through interest payments received on the mortgages they write. There are also a few hybrid REITs that provide loans to commercial real estate buyers and hold a portfolio of their own properties.

REIT Regulations

REITs must all meet certain annual requirements as required by the IRS. They must be managed by a board of directors. They must pay their shareholders a dividend that equals at least 90 percent of their taxable income. They must invest at least 75 percent of their assets in real estate assets. They must also derive at least 75 percent of their gross income from real estate property or from interest or mortgages on real property.

REIT ownership is also tightly regulated. All REITs are required to have a minimum of 100 shareholders, and no more than 50 percent of the shares may be held by five or fewer individuals.

Pros and Cons of REITS

Like all investments, REITs have some attractive advantages, as well as a few drawbacks.

On the downside, REITs are not particularly attractive for investors who are looking for capital appreciation. Since at least 90 percent of their taxable earnings are distributed to shareholders each year, their share value tends to change very little from year to year.

As a result, REITs may not be appropriate for investors who don't need or want income. The income they pay is fully taxable—so they can increase your annual tax burden unless you hold them in a tax-deferred retirement plan.

They also do carry some risk. In a down economy, if vacancies increase, you could see a drop in your income as well as in the share value of the REIT.

On the bright side, REITs can be an excellent investment for someone who wants to diversify beyond the typical stocks and bonds. They give you a stake in the real estate market and the steady income stream that goes with it. In fact, REITs offer among the highest dividends of any publicly traded investment, with returns often ranging between 5 and 12 percent. In fact, many REITs provide an increasing stream of income in a strong real estate market.

They are professionally managed by experts in the commercial real estate field who handle all the investments and property management for you.

Best of all, they offer small investors the opportunity to participate in the real estate market with a small cost of admission. If you were to buy commercial real estate on your own, it could cost you a significant amount of money. Participation in a limited partnership real estate deal could cost you $25,000 to $100,000 or more. But REITs give you the opportunity to pick your price. You can buy a few hundred dollars' worth of shares or a few thousand dollars' worth. You can invest whatever you can afford.

For convenience, outstanding income, diversification, and the opportunity to participate in the commercial real estate market, REITs can be an excellent investment for small and large investors alike.

Chapter 28

Forming and Operating a Real Estate Investment Trust

Provided for informational purposes only by Howard Edward Haller, Ph.D., a Licensed California Real Estate Broker.*

The following summarizes some of the basic U.S. tax law requirements applicable to REITs. These rules are complex and the following is a general summary only. To qualify as an REIT, an entity must meet many organizational, operational, distribution, and compliance requirements. If an REIT satisfies these requirements it will be entitled to deduct any dividends paid from its taxable income.

A REIT that distributes 100 percent of its taxable income therefore will have no federal income tax liability. Although state tax laws relating to REITs vary, most states with an income-based tax regime follow the federal law and permit an REIT a "dividends paid deduction."

There are Four Basic Tax Law Requirements:

- Organizational
- Operational
- Distribution
- Compliance

1. Organizational

An REIT must be formed in one of the fifty states or District of Columbia as a taxable entity for federal purposes as a corporation. It must be governed by directors or trustees, and its shares must be transferable.

Beginning in its second taxable year, an REIT must meet two ownership tests: it must have at least 100 different shareholders (the "100 Shareholder Test"), and five or fewer individuals cannot own more than 50 percent of the value of the REIT's stock during the last half of its taxable year (the "5/50 Test"). Many "look through" rules currently apply when determining whether the REIT meets the 5/50 Test. These ownership requirements generally mean that an REIT structure is not a good choice for a closely held family business.

To ensure compliance with these tests, most REITs include percentage ownership limitations in their organizational documents. For example, many REITs do not permit any one shareholder to own more than at most 9.9 percent of an REIT's stock without a waiver by the REIT's board of directors. Because of the need to have 100 shareholders and the complexity of both tests, general legal, and tax and securities law advice is strongly recommended prior to beginning the process of forming an REIT.

2. Operational

The REIT must satisfy two annual income tests and several quarterly asset tests that are designed to ensure that most of the REIT's income and assets are derived from real estate sources.

Annually, at least 75 percent of an REIT's gross income must come from real estate-related income such as rents from real property and interest on obligations secured by mortgages on real property. Though 95 percent of the REIT's gross income must be from the above-listed sources, 5 percent of the income can come from non-qualifying sources, such as service fees or other passive forms of income like dividends and interest from non-real estate sources (i.e. bank deposit interest).

An REIT can own up to 100 percent of the stock of a "taxable REIT subsidiary" ("TRS"), a corporation with which an REIT makes a joint election that can earn such income.

Quarterly, at least 75 percent of an REIT's assets must consist of real estate assets such as real property or loans secured by real property. Although an REIT can own up to 100 percent of a TRS, an REIT cannot own, directly or indirectly, more than 10 percent of the voting securities of any corporation other than another REIT, TRS, or qualified REIT subsidiary ("QRS"), a wholly owned subsidiary of the REIT whose assets and income are considered owned by the REIT for tax purposes. Nor can an REIT own stock in a corporation (other than an REIT, TRS, or QRS) whose stock value comprises more than 5 percent of an REIT's assets. Finally, the value of the stock of all an REIT's TRSs cannot comprise more than 25 percent of the value of the REIT's assets.

3. Distribution

To qualify, an REIT must distribute at least 90 percent of the sum of its taxable income. If the REIT retains income, it must pay tax on such income just as any other corporation.

4. Compliance

To qualify as an REIT, a company must make an REIT election by filing an income tax return on Form 1120-REIT. Because this form is not due until March 15th following the end of the REIT's tax year, the REIT does not make its election until after the end of its first year (or part-year) as an REIT. Nevertheless, if an REIT desires to qualify for the current year, it must meet the various REIT tests during that year (except for the 100 Shareholder Test and the 5/50 Test, both of which must be met beginning with the REIT's second taxable year).

Additionally, the REIT must annually mail letters to its shareholders of record, requesting details of beneficial ownership of shares. Significant monetary penalties will apply to an REIT that fails to mail these letters on a timely basis.

For a comprehensive review of the legal requirements of REITs, I recommend using the West Group's Legal Publication entitled: ***Real Estate Investment Trusts Handbook***.

*Disclaimer

This REIT Formation information is provided by Howard Edward Haller, Ph.D., an experienced and Licensed California Real Estate Broker, and is provided solely for informational purposes. It is not intended to constitute legal, accounting, real estate investing, or tax advice to the reader.

Because the formation and operation of an REIT involves many complex legal, securities, tax, and accounting rules, I strongly advise you to seek professional advice from competent securities and tax attorneys, **CPA**s, and other advisors prior to beginning the process of forming an **REIT**.

This is not legal advice. You should not rely upon any information contained herein for any purpose without seeking legal, real estate investing, and/or tax and accounting advice from a duly licensed attorney or tax practitioner.

Chapter 29

Is Commercial Real Estate a Good Choice for You?

Follow Your Dreams

Any investment is subject to the possibilities of cyclical changes. Each of the commercial property categories will have different factors influencing cash flow and appreciation potential. This is a positive feature that illustrates the ongoing value of portfolio diversification when an investor is searching for commercial real estate investment success.

This is an ideal time to invest in commercial real estate. Interest rates are low, rents are strong and increasing, and the long-term future looks excellent.

You could be like JD, who, as we discussed, at only twenty-four years old, purchased a nine-unit apartment building when he was out of work, with no current paycheck. He couldn't even qualify for a home.

Or Fred, who, with my help, bought a fifty-seven-unit apartment building with only $2,000 down, which he has since sold for mega bucks. He could replace the six-figure income from his day job (which shortly went away thereafter when the company he had been working for, for over ten years, collapsed. His job went away! Poof! Gone!) He has advanced to owning several apartment buildings in Florida and is living like a king on Vancouver Island.

Or Darryl, who is an established real estate broker who wanted to expand into the world of commercial real estate. With my help, he purchased $29 million worth of condos in Florida. He offered $13 million for the condos and was countered with $18 million, but also received 100 percent seller financing at only 3.3 percent interest.

You owe it to yourself to take the first steps in realizing your dream of becoming a commercial real estate owner. Get started today; visit:

https://www.commercialrealestatementor.org

Take care! ~Doc

CPSIA information can be obtained
at www.ICGtesting.com
Printed in the USA
FFOW02n0156180218
45074713-45461FF

9 781606 550366